T0362162

Gender, Emotions and Labour Markets

Concepts of emotion and emotional labour have largely been defined in European and American terms and according to Euro-American sensibilities with little attention given to the question of whether emotional work or emotional labour is different globally. In particular little has been written about the issue of what defines emotions and emotional labour in public work contexts and how it is configured in different cultural contexts. *Gender, Emotions and Labour Markets* considers how, and in what ways, emotional labour characterises formal and informal work environments in both Asia and the West. Key themes covered include: human rights issues and gender equity in formal and informal work contexts in Asia and the West; men, masculinity and emotional labour; impact on the work-life balance of professional women in Asian and Western contexts; the impact of the 'feminization of migration' in servicing high-end economic professionals; the impact of the new economy, organizational constraints on labour markets; and demographic patterns such as fertility, procreation, marriage, divorce in both Asian and Western contexts.

Ann Brooks is Professor of Sociology and Cultural Studies at the University of Adelaide. She is author of *Academic Women* (Open University Press,1997); *Postfeminisms: Feminism, Cultural Theory and Cultural Forms* (Routledge, 1997); and *Gendered Work in Asian Cities: The New Economy and Changing Labour Markets* (Ashgate, 2006). Her latest book is: *Social Theory in Contemporary Asia: Intimacy, Reflexivity and Identity* (Routledge 2010). Her forthcoming books include *Emotions in Transmigration: Transformation, Movement and Identity* (Palgrave 2011) and a co-edited collection (with David Lemmings) on the history of emotions in the work of Norbert Elias.

Theresa Devasahayam is Fellow and Gender Studies Programme Coordinator at the Institute of Southeast Asian Studies, Singapore. She is co-editor of *Working and Mothering in Asia: Images, Ideologies and Identities* (National University of Singapore Press 2007) and editor of *Gender Trends in Southeast Asia: Women Now, Women in the Future* (Institute of Southeast Asian Studies 2009).

Routledge Studies in Social and Political Thought

Gender, Emotions and Labour Markets

Asian and Western perspectives

Ann Brooks and Theresa Devasahayam

LONDON AND NEW YORK

First published 2011
by Routledge
2 Park Square, Milton Park, Abingdon, Oxon, OX14 4RN

Simultaneously published in the USA and Canada
by Routledge
711 Third Avenue, New York, NY 10017

Routledge is an imprint of the Taylor & Francis Group, an informa business

Typeset in Times New Roman by Swales & Willis Ltd, Exeter, Devon
Printed and bound by CPI Antony Rowe, Chippenham, Wiltshire

British Library Cataloguing in Publication Data
A catalogue record for this book is available from the British Library

Library of Congress Cataloging in Publication Data
Brooks, Ann, 1952–
    Gender, emotions and labour markets : Asian and Western perspectives /
    Ann Brooks and Theresa Devasahayam.
    p. cm. — (Routledge studies in social and political thought ; 72)
    Includes bibliographical references and index.
    1. Sex discrimination in employment—Asia.
    2. Women foreign workers—Asia—Social conditions.
    3. Women migrant labor— Asia—Social conditions.
    4. Women employment—Asia. I. Devasahayam, Theresa W. II. Title.
    HD6060.5.A78B76 2011
    331.4095—dc22
    2010027192

ISBN 13: 978-0-415-56389-5 (hbk)
ISBN 13: 978-0-203-83413-8 (ebk)

Contents

List of illustrations

Figures

Tables

Acknowledgements

The authors would like to acknowledge Professor Saskia Sassen, Columbia University, for her endorsement of this book. Ann Brooks would like to acknowledge the intellectual engagement and support for her work of two of the leading figures in Sociology globally, Professor John Scott in the UK and Professor Bryan Turner in the US. In Australia Ann wishes to acknowledge the friendship, enthusiasm and support of Professor David Lemmings who she is working with in the ARC Centre of Excellence in the History of Emotions which Professor Lemmings has recently established.

For publishing in the Social Sciences, publishing with Routledge is unrivalled. Its global outreach and outstanding lists making it the publisher of choice for those who wish their books to be listed with the best in the Social Sciences. For Ann Brooks this is the second book in 2010 within the Routledge Studies in Social and Political Thought Series. It has been a great pleasure to work with Peter Sowden, Senior Editor at Routledge over two books appearing in 2010 based within an Asian context. Peter is an excellent editor and a great enthusiast for scholarship in Asia. The authors would like to acknowledge the entire team at Routledge, including Emma Davis and Emma Hart who contributed to the book.

Professor Ann Brooks
Australia
November 2010

Introduction

Ann Brooks and Theresa Devasahayam

Contemporary theorizing on emotion and emotional labour

Ann Brooks

Late modernity has become conspicuously engaged with identity, reflexivity and emotions (Brooks 2008a; Brooks and Wee 2008; McNay 2008). This 'turn to affect' and emotions (Greco and Stenner 2008) in contemporary social theorizing and its increasing importance in broadening understanding in the social sciences is a response to a broader societal need. It is claimed that the model of 'an affective society' (Watson 1999) is now the predominant model. In fact, Greco and Stenner (2008:5) note that when emotion was directly addressed by the early social scientists 'it was typically associated with the primitive, the embodied female'. This book draws on conceptual frameworks around emotion to conceptualize a broader understanding of social processes involved in 'emotion work' and 'emotional labour' in the West and in Asia. The first part of this Introduction provides a theoretical framework for understanding emotional labour within the context of the West and Asia. The second part of the Introduction by Theresa Devasahayam provides an analysis of the social and cultural context of gender in Asia.

The 'affective turn' in the social sciences can be traced to the 1970s and 1980s with significant contributors to the theoretical shift including James Averill, Theodore Sarbin, Arlie Hochschild and Rom Harré, who advocated a 'social constructivist' approach to the study of emotions. These theorists, among others, advocated for a new subject matter in the social sciences around the emotions, which recognized a social and cultural context, rather than a purely scientific context as the basis for the new subject matter. As Greco and Stenner (2008: 8) note:

> [T]hese authors began to stress some of the very different ways in which emotions are played out intellectually among people from very different cultural backgrounds and the variety of ways in which they have been made sense of in different historical periods.

The conceptual significance of the term 'emotion' and the distinction between the concepts 'emotion' and 'affect' is shown in the way the concept provides synergy between the scientific and social scientific discourses as follows (ibid.: 12):

The term 'emotion' entered into circulation as part of a medico-scientific discourse associated with the early development of scientific psychology. In calling affective life 'emotion' these novel scientific discourses also transformed the ways in which people thought about their affective life specifically, the emotions came to be thought of as quasi-mechanical biological processes.

The late entry of the social sciences into the study of emotions has had some positive effects. Some social theorists (Clough 2007; Massumi 2002; Sedgwick 2003) introduced innovative agendas which built on the successes of the natural and clinical sciences. Beyond this, social scientists have also drawn on these concepts to understand the way social relations are conducted. As Greco and Stenner (2008: 14) comment (see also Brooks 2010):

> Social scientists have examined the dissemination of psy-concepts and the social conspicuousness of emotion talk within the context of rationalities of government that increasingly rely on reflexive forms of self-management and self-regulation on the part of individuals. . . . At a more general level, this development has been addressed in terms of processes of *individualization* (Beck 1992) and *reflexive modernization* (Beck, Giddens and Lash 1994; Castells 2004; Giddens 1992).

The relationship between emotion and affect is important and as Greco and Stenner (2008: 16) note, affect is a central concept in understanding contemporary economic processes including 'emotional labour' in the service industry. In addition, Hochschild's (2008) work on emotions emphasizes the importance of a process of interaction which acts between the personality structures of individuals and social structures. In her article, 'Emotion Work, Feeling Rules and Social Structures' (2008), Hochschild shows how 'emotion work' enables us to connect emotions to broader questions of power and social structure, and the gendered relationships which emerge (see Fineman 2005; Fisher and Ashkanasy 2000; Lewis and Simpson 2007).

Key concepts in the sociology of emotions

There is a well-established literature in the US and Europe around the area of 'emotional labour' (Hochschild 1983) or 'emotion work' (Hochschild 1990, 2003a, 2003b, 2005) where 'emotions' in the workplace are conceptualized as managing the emotions of others or undertaking labour which accommodates the emotional demands made on women in a formal or informal work environment. Much of the seminal work on emotions and emotional labour has involved the theorizing of emotions within organizational settings. Hochschild's (1983) research on flight attendants (mostly female) in the airline industry has a central place in organizational emotion theory (Fineman 2000), other work includes Martin *et al.*'s (1998) work on the Body Shop, which explores the notion of 'bounded emotionality' in a for-profit organization staffed and managed by a high proportion of women, and

P. J. Frost's (2004, 2007) work on toxic emotions at work. Other work includes Blair-Loy (2003) and Blair-Loy and Jacobs (2003) on stockbrokers and the 'care deficit'.

The concept of emotional labour has largely emerged from the analysis of organizations in the West, and the concept of management which has played a key role in the framing of the debate has been tied to ideas about masculinity (Hatcher 2003). The emotional labour debate has been contextualized within an analysis of the modern organization that defines managerial attributes as confident, assertive and empowered (Clegg *et al.* 1995; Koller 2004). So-called 'feminine' emotions such as caution, anxiety, caring are often evaluated negatively (Ashforth and Humphrey 1995).

Other work has focused on a broader definition of emotional labour within the process of migration and includes the work undertaken on 'global care chains' (Hochschild 1989, 1997, 2003a, 2003b; Hondagneu-Sotelo 2001; Salazar Parreñas 2001a, 2001b). Theorizing the links between globalization, global capital, and the servicing of high-end economic migrants by female migrant labour, Brooks (2006) has provided a model to encapsulate the situation in Southeast Asia.

Emotion work and emotional labour

This Introduction provides a brief theoretical and conceptual backdrop of research into emotions, emotion work and emotional labour. Emotional labour (Hochschild 1983) or 'emotion work' (Hochschild 1993) is conceptualized as managing the emotions of others or undertaking labour which accommodates the emotional demands made on women in a formal or informal work environment. In the context of this book we will use the term 'emotional labour'.

Emotional labour has largely been defined in European and American terms and according to Euro-American sensibilities. Little thought has been given to the question of whether emotional work or emotional labour is different globally and in what ways. Cross-cultural comparisons tend to be drawn on to confirm already established understandings rather than to highlight any differences. The debate continues in the West about the issue of emotional labour (Hochschild 2003b; Meyer 2000) and its significance for gender equity within and outside formal and informal structures. However, little has been written about the issue of what defines emotional labour and how it is configured in different cultural contexts. This book addresses that gap in the literature and considers how and in what ways emotional labour characterizes formal and informal work environments in the West and Asia.

Despite several international statutes on gender equity and human rights such as the Convention on the Elimination of all forms of Discrimination Against Women (CEDAW) (1979), major barriers continue to restrict women's rights and behaviour in the workplace in Asia and elsewhere. Emotional labour has not been analysed there in the same way as in the West. This book addresses this issue. The debates are set in the context of contemporary theorizing around gender, patterns of labour migration, the 'feminization' of labour and the 'feminization' of migration', labour force participation (LFP), formal and informal organizational structures, new economy debates, debates on men and masculinities, caregiving and parenting, and human rights in Asia.

There has been little in the way of feminist critiques of the emotional labour literature. One of the more challenging critiques from anti-racist and feminist theory comes from Mirchandani (2003, 2008). Her critique focuses on the 'racial silences' in the literature on emotion work as well as a critique of dominant methodological approaches. She claims that research in the area of 'emotion work' relies on racially homogenous samples, which assume workers are white. Similarly Pierce's 1995 study of female paralegals examines how Asian, African or Hispanic paralegals (or attorneys) would change the situation. Pierce's work also highlights the racialized nature of such environments. Steinberg and Figart (1999: 17–18) show that there are cultural assumptions with implicit gendered and racial discourses characterizing both emotional labour work and research in the field:

> In the United States, for example, where service organizations emphasize emotional displays of friendliness, women are more likely to be hired to work in these organizations because it is believed that, on average they smile and display more warmth than men do. Yet in Muslim culture, such displays are restricted by employees because they would provoke a sexual response.

While the work undertaken in Asia has considered the implications of global care chains (Devasahayam and Yeoh 2007; Litt and Zimmerman 2003; Yeoh *et al.* 1999), there has been little explicit analysis of emotional labour or emotion work in the context of Asia, or the racialized aspects of the work undertaken by migrant female domestic labour. There are of course different forms of emotional labour and emotion work linked to migration including: transmigrant marriages, transmigrant entertainment and sex work, and transmigration of female domestic workers. This latter group form the largest of these transmigrant groupings. The transmigration of female labour has traditionally been seen as a largely exploitative process, which has been seen as synonymous with human trafficking. However, the agency of transmigrant female labour is now seen to be more diversified and complex (Hilsdon 2007; Nakamatsu 2005b). While the authors are specifically focusing on emotional labour in the context of female migrant domestic labour, consideration will also be given to these other forms of emotion work.

Aims of the book

The aims of the book are as follows:

- to examine the emotional labour debate in the West and in the context of Asia;
- to set the debates within the context of debates around globalization, labour force participation, emotions and gender equity within the West and in Asia;
- to examine caregiving, parenting and emotional labour for both professional women and female migrant domestic workers in the West and in Asia;
- to consider the work–life balance of professional women in the US and the Asia-Pacific;

- to examine the impact of the 'feminization of migration';
- to examine the servicing of 'high-end' economic migrants and local populations in Asia and the West;
- to assess human rights issues in the context of female migrant labour in Asia;
- to examine men, masculinity and emotional labour.

Social and cultural context of gender and emotional labour in Asia

Theresa Devasahayam

The impact of economic modernity and accompanying debates on emotional labour, gender equity and gender differentiation can be seen in the discourses on gender and emotional labour in Asia. Contemporary Asian women have, in the main, been successful in reconciling 'modernity' with 'tradition'. To be modern for these women means to be able to contribute actively to the economies of their countries. The emphasis of governments in the region to include women as an economic force in countries such as Singapore, Malaysia and Vietnam (see Brooks 2010) has had a significant impact on women's status. Entering the job market has been made possible because of the expanding economies in the region which have created vast numbers of jobs in the electronics, textile, clerical, service, teaching and nursing sectors. This trend, coupled with a 'revolution in gender balance in educational opportunities' marked by the numbers of women overtaking men receiving tertiary-level education, has enabled women to take on higher-status jobs in the workforce (Jones 2003, 2009a: 14).

The lives of women with low levels of education have also been transformed in recent decades. Rural women have also been pushed into wage employment as a result of mechanization replacing human labour on farms although often these women take on unskilled or low-skilled work whether in cities or abroad because their governments have not been able to produce non-farm work quickly enough (Devasahayam 2009a; Elmhirst 2008; Stahl 2003). In many cases, these women take on jobs as temporary migrant workers in the domestic work sector in Malaysia, Hong Kong and Saudi Arabia.

The picture on the ground, however, has been diverse and more nuanced. In some instances, Asian women have appeared to have been successfully able to liberate themselves altogether from the grip of tradition by choosing to have smaller families or even avoiding marriage completely. But for the majority of married women, they face the task of taking on wage work without abandoning traditional expectations of their role as women in the household. The general consensus in the Asian region is that women have the liberty to work as long as they continue to be the primary caregivers in the familial context (see Brooks 2010). What this means for them is that they are confronted with having to balance the two worlds of wage work and care work (Devasahayam and Yeoh 2007).

While in the past, marriage was a near universal trend, increasingly there has been a marked shift toward a delay in, or even rejection of marriage throughout the region. Countries in Asia, demonstrating the trend toward delayed marriage include Japan, Thailand, Myanmar, Singapore, Malaysia, Taiwan, the Philippines, and, to a lesser extent, South Korea and Indonesia (Brooks 2010; Jones 2004). But there are variations according to region within countries. It has been shown that delayed marriage tends to be an urban more than a rural phenomenon (Jones 2009a). The pattern of delayed marriage and the emphasis on 'singlehood' has been comprehensively explored by Brooks (2010).

There are many reasons for this demographic shift. Structural changes by way of changing education and work patterns among women have been implicated as critical factors since they enable financial independence by women. In this regard, the idea that marriage leads to financial security no longer carries the import it once had. Moreover, childbearing as an expected outcome of marriage has lost its significance while in some countries pregnancy is no longer tied to marriage, suggesting that the link between childbearing and marriage is changing (Raymo and Iwasawa 2008). These past trends have changed as women become active contributors to the household income, a trend that is inevitable because of rising costs of living (Devasahayam 2010).

Especially among highly-educated women, a career has become more important than raising a family (see Jones 2003, 2004). Among them, children are accorded a lower status and perceived to be a disincentive to marriage since they are viewed as a potential disruption to career and a factor for the loss of independence (Brooks 2010; Jones 2009a; McDonald 2009; Nemoto 2008). But it must be noted that the link between the pursuit of a career and fertility has been questioned. Hirao (2007) cites figures demonstrating that the fertility rate between working married women and stay-at-home mothers shows little difference. Parents unconsciously contribute to non-marriage. For women residing with their parents – a common living arrangement in Asia – it was found that larger financial transfers to parents have been associated with delayed marriage (Raymo and Ono 2007), suggesting that women are willing to set aside their own desires and instead prioritize the needs of their elderly parents (see also Jones 2003). In this regard, some women might actually see this role as resisting gender inequality (Nemoto 2008) since it takes them away from a potential marital partnership which does not have much to offer (Jones 2003).

As in delayed marriage, non-marriage as a demographic phenomenon has also been noticeable in the Asian region. Climbing steadily in the region, the incidence of non-marriage among women in the 40–44 cohort is highest in Japan, South Korea, and Myanmar, with the Philippines, Thailand and Indonesia following the same pattern (Jones 2004, 2007). The strongest factor for non-marriage is education, with the vast majority of non-married women having higher levels of education as opposed to women with lower levels of education. Jones (2004) emphasizes that lower proportions of higher educated women marry into their thirties and forties compared with lower-educated women although delayed and non-marriage has been evident in both educational cohorts.

Evidence from Japan reveals that extended school enrolment leads to later marriage (Raymo 2003), suggesting a change in values among the younger generation of women. Especially among highly-educated women, non-marriage is an inevitable outcome since it becomes increasingly difficult for them to find suitable partners given that hypogamy continues to be practised with men dominating the 'buyer's market' (Lyons-Lee 1998: 315) as they seek out less educated and younger partners (Jones 2009a; Raymo and Iwasawa 2005). Some governments have also shown concern over the non-marriage of 'graduate women' defining it specifically as a problem (Lyons-Lee 1998).

Interestingly, the inverse is true of men where it is low educational levels that are linked to non-marriage, presumably because lowly-educated men hold a low status in the marriage market coupled with the fact that their economic situation deters them from forming a family (Jones 2007). For a growing number of them, especially from the more affluent countries, seeking a foreign bride, particularly from the economically disadvantaged countries in the region, has become an option (Jones and Shen 2008).

But the picture is even more complex. In some countries such as in Japan, the image of the self-sacrificial mother has lost its appeal and mothering has become increasingly bound up with choice rather than duty (Hirao 2007). Moreover given the close association between marriage and children, avoiding having children would mean avoiding marriage in the first place (Jones 2009a, 2009b). The demands of parenting have also proved to be a critical factor for non-marriage. In Japan, couples are expected to produce 'high quality' children (Hirao 2007: 54), putting pressure mainly on women to engage in 'intensive parenting' since they are the primary caregivers in the family (Jones 2009a: 22), thus discouraging the younger generation of women from entering marriage. Besides there is evidence that satisfaction associated with raising children has diminished because of anxiety, distress, discontent and lack of self-confidence (Hirao 2007).

The response has been that women are opting out of marriage. That inequality persists in the division of labour in the household has prompted women to retreat from marriage (Jones 2004, 2009b). Particularly among educated women, the inability to find partners who hold similar values on attitudes toward shared housework and childrearing has been a crucial factor for non-marriage (Hull 2002, as cited in Jones 2009a; Raymo and Ono 2007). Even if there is agreement on the need for greater sharing of housework and care work, as is shown in Japanese surveys, there appears to be a disjuncture between attitude and behaviour since these tasks continue to be largely left to women (Hirao 2007).

As in the West, the lack of government policies to help women balance work demands and family commitments has reduced the 'desirability of marriage' (Jones 2004: 17) for women, although the 'trade-offs between labour market work and family . . . are felt most strongly by women in the lower middle income ranges, who cannot afford to employ a maid'(ibid.: 18). Besides, in this globalized world, finding employment abroad has become commonplace. But working abroad for long stretches of time has its own disadvantages such as delayed marriage for the single woman.

With non-marriage increasingly looked upon as an option, this has been argued to have taken a toll on fertility rates in Asia (Jones 2003, 2004, 2007, 2009b). Other factors cited for the declining fertility rates in East Asia in particular are:

difficulties encountered in work–family balance; perceived economic risk in raising a family among younger adults; and the lack of government and employer measures to support the family (McDonald 2009). The trend in the latter part of the last century has been a slow fertility decline starting with the high-income countries in the region such as Japan, Hong Kong and South Korea, a pattern which is now emerging in the less developed countries (Jones 2009b). In Southeast Asia, fertility declines have been coupled with low fertility (approximately replacement level or even below), a demographic trend found among the ethnic Chinese and Indians (for example, in Singapore and Malaysia), Myanmar, Thailand, Vietnam, and most of Indonesia (Jones 2009a). It has been argued that the anti-natalist policies in some countries have been responsible for the declining fertility rates in the past few decades. China is a good example (see Jones 2009b for details). But measures to reverse such policies have had little success in turning the situation around because they have been implemented too late (McDonald 2002, as cited in Chan and Yeoh 2002; Ogawa 2002; as cited in Chan and Yeoh 2002; Jones *et al.* 2009a). Singapore is one such example (Jones *et al.* 2009a).

Governments in East and Southeast Asia are expecting the trend of declining fertility to continue for some time (Jones *et al.* 2009b). Declining fertility rates have led some Asian governments to turn to migration to meet the needs of an ever expanding labour market. The fast greying populations of countries such as Japan and Singapore have had the same outcome. Invariably economic growth disparities between countries in the region have spurred the movement of people mainly from the poorer economies to the more affluent ones. In Asia, Brunei Darussalam, Hong Kong, Japan, Singapore, South Korea and Taiwan figure as major magnets for both skilled as well as unskilled labour migrants. Major labour-sending economies include the Philippines for both skilled and unskilled labour while Indonesia, Sri Lanka, India and Nepal are noted for their export of unskilled labour. The export of labour has become a major source of revenue for many labour-sending countries compared with non-trade sources. For this reason, many export labour economies in the Asian region gain huge benefits from ensuring that the migration channels are kept open (Asian Development Outlook 2009). While there has been considerable regional cooperation to avoid protectionist policies, however, there has been less effort to ensure the rights of these migrants (ibid.).

Although past migration trends demonstrate that more men than women migrants sought work abroad, the numbers of female migrants worldwide has been steadily growing leading to what has been termed the feminization of migration. The Asian region is no exception (Huguet 2003; Piper 2004a). That large numbers of women have been seeking wage work abroad reflects their emancipation from the domestic sphere and empowerment as a result of wage work – a phenomenon which would have never occurred in the past as males were seen to be the breadwinners in the family.

While there are skilled women migrants, the vast majority are unskilled workers (Chia 2008). Because there are more obstacles in obtaining employment abroad for unskilled work particularly for men, women have been forced to migrate for employment, often taking over the breadwinner role from men (Salazar Parreñas

2005). Among many rural households, adversity and poverty are drivers for labour migration as a means of survival (Resurreccion 2009). Moreover, relatively few cultural constraints exist to constrain the mobility of women especially in Southeast Asia (Resurreccion 2009).

But the kinds of jobs women take on are indicative of women's inferior status in the global labour market. The majority of women migrants are employed in 'feminized work' in the domestic work, caregiving and entertainments sectors which result in many being lowly paid and being ascribed low status (Jolly and Reeves 2005; Tan 2001, as cited in Huguet 2003). Clearly, engaging in feminized work reflects the gender stereotyping prevalent in the global economy. But poor women leave their countries to secure employment in the more affluent countries where there is demand for domestic and care work because women in the labour-receiving countries rather pursue careers while transferring their own domestic demands to foreign women, a trend which suggests that the cultural expectations of women as the primary caregivers in the family continue to be strong. For this reason, women undertake the kinds of work already determined as inferior labourers in the labour market (Pearson 1997), and not necessarily as 'natural . . . bearers of inferior labour' (Resurreccion 2009: 32).

But it is curious how gender is reproduced in other ways at different levels across Asia. In the past few decades, religion in particular has been a great force bolstering conservative notions of women's role in the family. Trends in religion in Southeast Asia, for example, show a growing inclination toward fundamentalism, pushing women further into traditional roles. Such values have been promoted in different contexts. White (2006: 277, 276) points out how a handbook from a girls' *pesantren* in Solo mandates that a Muslim woman 'surrender[s] all the affairs of her life to the law and sharia of God' and 'remains mainly in the home, in accordance with her nature (*fitroh*) and duties'.

Women's bodies have also been the site of Islamic fundamentalism (Rinaldo 2008). Islamic clerics in Malaysia and Indonesia have been insisting on the veiling of women, arguing that it represents female purity. The rise of conservative Islamic forces is also revealing in the contexts of conversion and marriage where only women's behaviour and appearance have become delimited and rigorously defined especially in Indonesia and Malaysia (Mohammad 2009). In this case, increasing Islamization cannot be divorced from state politics (Ong 1995). The influence of religion on government policy is also evidenced in the Philippines. Here, women's bodies have become the site of contestation when the state advocates the Roman Catholic Church dogma on the use of contraceptives (Austria 2004). Although the state might not overtly promote conservative notions of women's role in the family, by placing limits on women's sexuality, it invariably promotes a pro-natalist position and, in turn, women's caregiver role in the family since the bulk of this work is carried out by women.

Overview of the book

In Chapter 1, 'Globalization, labour force participation and the gender gap' Theresa Devasahayam provides a comprehensive review of the relationship between globalization, labour force participation and the gender gap. It documents the positive as well as the negative economic and social effects of globalization on workers, especially female workers, in Southeast Asia. Although globalization has opened up more jobs in many countries (Dunn and Skaggs 1999), women in particular have been marginalized in five respects: (1) the formal sector of the economy; (2) the gendered division of labour; (3) the exploitative nature of multinational corporations; (4) the double burden women face; and (5) the negative effects of structural adjustment programmes of international financial institutions (Devasahayam and Yeoh 2007; Hensman 1996; Hippert 2002; Jagger 2001; Kawewe and Dibie 2000; Mills 2003; Sassen 2000). In exploring the extent of globalization's impact on the gender gap in the economy and women's labour force participation, the argument here is that in spite of women's continuing economic contribution, their efforts have failed to improve the unequal relationship between men and women prevalent in the labour force because of structural, political, economic and social factors that place constraints on their empowerment through work.

The concept of labour force participation (LFP) has long been employed because of its value in explaining why certain groups are employed in specific sectors. Specifically women's labour force participation rate refers to the ratio of their participation in the labour force vis-à-vis the total population. Labour force participation is generally determined by wage rates, changing attitudes to women taking up wage employment, women's educational level, delayed marriage, and low birthrates. Global indicators for women's employment, which include status, sector and wage earnings, may also be applied to Asian women, with men more likely than women to be employed in formal, salaried work, and with women more likely than men to earn less for the same type of work.

While women in Asia have contributed heavily to the economic growth of the region, they are caught in a bind because their engagement in the labour market has mostly been regarded as complementary to the work men do and thus accorded secondary economic value (Devasahayam and Yeoh 2007). By filling certain kinds of jobs targeted at them, whether in the countries of their home origin or across the countries in the region, they are unable to mitigate gender inequality and are forced to conceal and, in turn, reinforce, either consciously or unconsciously, the structural, social and cultural constructs bolstered by patriarchal ideologies that define their role and identity as women.

The asymmetrical relationship between men and women in the labour market is evident in work opportunities, experiences, rewards and challenges. While paid work may be taken as an indicator of women's progress (Clark *et al.* 1991; Young *et al.* 1996), there persists a gender gap evidenced in men earning more than women, holding higher management positions than women, dominating the more lucrative jobs, and having greater access to work in the formal sector. Generally, the factors for the persistence of the gender gap are related to employment and earnings opportunities and to the opportunity costs of not working.

In Chapter 2, 'Changing patterns of caregiving and emotional labour in Asia', Devasahayam and Brooks explore the issue of emotional labour in Asia in the context of indigenous ideologies and government policies in Asia. The aim of this chapter is to show that for working mothers the act of balancing the worker and caregiver roles is fraught with tensions because of cultural and social norms that continue to be strong, while at the same time economic growth policies of countries are demanding that women work.

Some women have been fortunate enough to appropriate strategies to integrate the two worlds of workplace and home by resorting to institutional care whether state-sponsored or privately run childcare centres. In the industrialized countries of the Western hemisphere, the increasing availability of institutionalized childcare arrangements and part-time work has made it possible for women to take on paid work (Bernhardt 1993; England 1996). The experience of Asian women has been different as they have the option of relying on informal childcare arrangements such as neighbours, grandparents and other relatives (Huang and Yeoh 1997; Yeoh and Huang 1995). Others have been able to purchase care work through the services rendered by other women. In Malaysia and Singapore, for example, women from the poorer countries in Southeast Asia provide domestic service in the more affluent countries, thereby replacing the domestic role of local women who then enter the labour force (Litt and Zimmerman 2003; Yeoh *et al.* 1999).

The chapter explores a range of examples from countries in Asia which show how ideology combined with policy has led to anxiety over appropriate identities for women while frequently leaving men out of the discourses on family and fertility. Legal discourses highlight the ambiguous position in which women are frequently located in relation to being economically productive yet maintaining expected roles as caregivers.

The focus of Chapter 3, 'Globalization, the feminization of migration and emotional labour', by Theresa Devasahayam is on how Southeast Asia has become a nucleus for the feminization of migration with countries in the region becoming increasingly absorbed into the global economy (Huguet 2003; Piper 2004a). The region has become a hotbed for transnational female labour flows in recent decades (Wong *et al.* 2003).

Because of labour shortages as a result of falling fertility rates and a fast-growing ageing population, some Asian countries have had little choice but to depend on foreign labour from countries in the region whose populations have surplus labour.

This chapter explores the experiences of women migrants in their effort to 'uproot' and 'reground' themselves in their efforts to negotiate their multiple identities to make sense of their reality in the destination economies (Ahmed *et al.* 2004). It shows that in spite of engaging in paid work, the demands of carrying out the nurturer and caregiver role persist for migrant women because of the kinds of jobs they take, since these jobs continue to emphasize women's caring and nurturing roles. Furthermore, women migrants continue to operate within a context of emotions. Like women from the developed countries who take on jobs in the formal work sector dominated by men, they face similar contradictions. Unskilled migrant women are expected to be detached from their own families and to concentrate their emotional energies toward the betterment of their 'workplace family'.

Some women are also expected to completely shed their identity as mothers – an identity which they carry with them in their experience as migrant workers because it is primarily their families that have provided the impetus for them to migrate for work in the first place. Paradoxically, although the majority engage in care work, their capacity to engage fully in this kind of work is curtailed by their worker identity since their identities as workers are emphasized above their identities as mothers. While the constraints they face are not very different from women who stay behind with their families, there is the added tension of having to carry out their nurturer role at a distance in spite of being physically separated from their families. While this might be the experience of unskilled/low-skilled women workers, skilled women workers who migrate for work are subject to the same rules because the workplace tends to be male-dominated.

As such, women who migrate for work, whether skilled or unskilled/low-skilled, have a heavy price to pay in their own families, as this chapter demonstrates. The bulk of women who migrate for wage work are mothers but who are not privileged to bring their children along with them to the countries they find work. While their own children are deprived of their love, these women find themselves giving their love to the children of the families in which they work (Hochschild 2003b).

But women migrants are not victims in the migration process, as this chapter argues. Instead whether unskilled/low-skilled or skilled, they have been found to exercise agency in the choices they have undertaken and, to use a term coined by de Certeau (1984), to 'make meaning' in their migration experiences albeit with constraints in some circumstances.

In Chapter 4, 'Human rights and female migrant labour in Asia', Theresa Devasahayam shows that migration throws up complex situations, both of opportunity and risk for the individuals who decide to migrate for work. Here, employment abroad is a two-edged sword: while leaving one's country to work in another opens up opportunities for improvement for one's family, female as well as male migrant workers alike are vulnerable to a range of abuses over which they have very little control.

In spite of pleas on the part of sending countries to ask receiving country governments to enact relevant measures and policies to protect their own migrating citizens, the governments of many receiving destinations in the Asian region have been slow in reacting to the need to protect foreign nationals (Piper 2004b; Yeoh *et al.* 2004). In addition, the lack of regional frameworks to protect migrant rights has been limited (Chia 2008).

This chapter demonstrates that the social construction of migrant workers as 'non-citizens' underpin the abuses they experience because the relationship between rights and citizenship appears to be increasingly delinked in spite of expanding labour flows in the global economy (Castles and Davidson 2000). But there is an added complexity to the experience of unskilled migrant workers based on gender, beyond being non-citizens in the receiving countries. In some countries, labour laws serve to marginalize unskilled female foreign workers while privileging the male foreign worker populace (Huang and Yeoh 2003). That they are 'temporary' to the labour-receiving countries need not be a significant factor for the lack of protection of their rights since the majority of unskilled male migrants are also considered temporary workers although both groups may stay on for periods much longer than their initial contract.

Instead this chapter argues that it is the nature of the work engaged in by women migrants that increases their vulnerability to abuses with limited access to solution. Migrant women tend to engage in work intimately linked to their caring and nurturing role and, therefore, considered peripheral to the formal economy by all the migration stakeholders, from states and employers to migrant brokers and others in the migration labour chain, unlike men's work and, concomitantly, labour. For this reason, the stakes are high for women migrants who have been left with little protection apart from having to either fend for themselves or rely on non-governmental efforts to improve their work conditions (Piper 2003).

A growing concern in the region with the large waves of especially unskilled women within and across countries is the issue of trafficking (Gallagher 2005). On the one hand, while being caught in conditions shaped by structural, social and cultural expectations that impel women to migrate to find work to help their own families, the lack of adequate social and human capital on the other has increased their vulnerability to being victims of human trafficking. Because so few mechanisms are in place to check the trafficking of women, especially into the flesh trade, Devasahayam shows how Third World women in Southeast Asia have found themselves being confronted by patriarchy head-on as victims of sexual abuse.

In Chapter 5, Ann Brooks examines 'Women executives and emotional labour: the work–life balance of professional women in the Asia-Pacific and the US'. She shows how globalization is fundamentally restructuring traditional labour markets and the way in which individuals are redefining their market position and their identity. She discusses how the global economy, often reinforced in state discourses, positions women in an ambiguous and contradictory position in regard to economic discourses and public policies.

Brooks notes how there has been virtually no research on how specific pressures of the global economy affect the prospects for caregiving among highly skilled, well-heeled First World professionals (Blair-Loy and Jacobs 2003). These high-end 'servants of globalization' (Salazar Parreñas 2001a) face a range of new pressures from increased competition, workplace and time deadlines. High-ranking professional women, like their male colleagues, face workplace cultures that assume elite employees will put in very long hours on an uninterrupted and full-time basis, even during the family formative years (Epstein *et al.* 1999; Williams 2000). Yet most women lack support from a spouse at home (Brooks 2006; Catalyst 2001; Hochschild 1997; Wajcman 1996).

In this chapter, Ann Brooks reviews professional women in a range of occupations to discuss the obstacles they confront within formal and informal organizational structures and domestic contexts surrounding emotional labour and assesses the impact on their careers and their marriages. Brooks provides a range of examples of case studies and literature from the Asia-Pacific and the US. Drawing on

Hochschild's (1997, 2003a, 2003b, 2005) work to theorize the position of professional women regarding emotional labour demands, Brooks balances a range of theoretical and empirical research to illuminate the significance of emotional labour in the work–life balance of professional women globally.

In Chapter 6, 'Servicing high-end professional populations: Female migrant labour as a transnational community', Ann Brooks shows how the transmigration of labour is used to service the emotional labour demands of professional workers. Brooks shows how globalization has created strategic sites where a number of global processes intersect (Sassen 1998). These processes include the 'feminization of labour', the role of knowledge work, and the functionality of different groups of knowledge workers in the process. Within the global economy, knowledge and knowledge workers have become a significant element of transnational migration at the high end, with high incomes and designer lifestyles. These groups put a high demand on a range of services supplied by transnational migration at the lower end. As Sassen (ibid.: 9) notes:

> The expansion of the high-income workforce in conjunction with the emergence of new cultural forms has led to a process of high-income gentrification that rests, in the last analysis, on the availability of a vast supply of low wage workers . . . the immigrant woman serving the white middle class professional woman has replaced the traditional image of the black female servant serving the white master.

The labour-intensive nature of high-income gentrification is an important aspect of the emergence of global cities. It is a pattern which characterizes many of the global cities of Southeast Asia. In the context of global restructuring, what feminists and other theorists call the 'feminization of labour' refers not only to the unprecedented increase in the number of women workers in the formal (and informal) labour force to service the global economy but also to the 'flexibilization' and 'casualization' of (especially women's) labour to keep costs down and productivity up.

Transnational labour migration is a feature of globalization which has become increasingly 'feminized'. Southeast Asia has become an important site for labour migration with Hong Kong, Taiwan and Malaysia and Singapore being key destinations for female foreign domestic workers (Cheng 1996; Chiang 2000; Chin 1998; Huang and Yeoh 1997; Tan 1999; Wong 1996). This chapter examines the 'maid culture' of Southeast Asia servicing the emotional needs of high-end migrants and local populations in global cities in Southeast Asia. It examines the implications of the dependency on maids and draws on the work of Aihwa Ong (2006) who offers a number of explanations for the abuse and degradation of female transmigrant workers, and who argues that they are treated as 'biopolitical others'.

In Chapter 7, 'Men, masculinity and emotional labour' Ann Brooks considers the issue of masculinity and emotional labour. She shows how an increasing emphasis is being given to the relationship between men, masculinity and emotional labour. The provision and expansion of services around emotional labour have applied mainly to executives and professionals, both single men and women and what Sassen (2003) has called 'professional households without wives'. Demographic factors have given greater emphasis to the issue of emotional labour as regards parenting responsibilities. Hochschild (2003a) notes that in most of the advanced industrial world, the divorce rate has risen and with it the number of single parent families. Most single parents are women and divorced men provide much less care for their children than married men. Hochschild also notes that a national survey in the US shows that half of American divorced fathers had not visited their children for over a year and provided no child support. Wealthy divorced fathers were just as likely to be negligent as poor fathers.

Reay (2004: 59) shows that within families, women engage in emotional labour far more than most men, taking responsibility for maintaining the emotional aspects of family relationships, responding to others' emotional states and also acting to alleviate distress. Adkins (2002) notes that an increasing number of men may be appropriating femininity and feminine ways of being in order to increase their mobility in the labour market, however, Reay (2004) comments that in the domestic sphere there seems to be a 'fixity' of outlook around who does the mothering, with women still taking responsibility for the majority of emotional labour. Thus, as Coltrane and Galt (2000) note, the gendered division of family care work remains the norm, despite the fact that men have been doing more in the home. Mothers are still more likely than fathers to take time off from their jobs to provide continuous childcare, spending significantly more time than fathers in all aspects of parenting.

Within an organizational context, Hearn (1994), Morgan (1992) and Gheradi (1995) have challenged the gender neutrality of work in organizational studies which rendered gender differences invisible. Organizations still operate as arenas characterized by male normative standards which frequently create a hostile working environment for minority groups such as women. However, men working in female-dominated occupations have been found to benefit from their token status (Bradley 1993; Williams 1993) through the assumption of leadership and other skills. Simpson (2004), in a study of men in female-dominated occupations, notes that men adopt a variety of strategies to re-establish a 'masculinity' that has been undermined by the 'feminine' nature of the work. So any additional expenditure of emotional labour which emerges from these areas of work is offset by strategies such as re-labelling, status enhancement and distancing from the feminine (Heikes 1992; Lupton 2002; Simpson 2004).

Research into career-oriented couples (Blair-Loy 2001, 2003; Blair-Loy and Jacobs 2003; Hochschild 2003a; Williams 2000) highlights the issues confronting women, particularly female executives who work long hours and who frequently find themselves unsupported by their spouse. As Blair-Loy (2003: 166) comments:

> The new delegatory model of motherhood remains gendered and hierarchical. When a family's nurturing needs exceed what can be purchased, it remains the women's responsibility to make sure the nurturing gets done. The exhausting emotional and practical labour of caring for the family through difficult

times is still shouldered by even career dedicated, high earning women at the expense of their professional callings.

In this chapter, Ann Brooks examines the relationship of men, masculinity and emotional labour across both organizational and domestic spheres and assesses the implications for changes in the nature of the relationship between men and emotional labour.

In this book, the authors Ann Brooks and Theresa Devasahayam explore the ramifications of debates around emotional labour in the West and in Asia and consider the implications for the gendered division of labour in both parts of the world.

1 Globalization, labour force participation and the gender gap

Theresa Devasahayam

Introduction

Asia has undergone rapid economic growth in the past few decades, issuing phrases such as the 'the East Asian Miracle', 'the Asian Era' and 'Rising Asia'. East Asia has seen the highest rate of economic growth at 6.1 per cent in comparison to all other regions in the world according to 2009 estimates (International Labour Organization 2010). The burgeoning economy of China has had positive spill-over effects on the countries in the region and thereby has been critical in sustaining relative high levels of economic growth. Although showing much slower growth rates for the same year owing to the economic meltdown, Southeast Asia has long been recognized as a fast developing region in the world, accompanied by impressive economic growth indicators. Strong levels of growth have been attributed to high savings rate, the creation of human capital, market reforms, the role of state intervention, cultural ideologies, namely the Confucian ethic, and the emergence of labour-intensive export manufacturing industries (Kaur 2004).

Since the 1960s, industrialization has made firm headway in East Asia and Southeast Asia. Government intervention has largely been credited with the rapid and sustained economic growth of Japan, South Korea and Singapore. In Southeast Asia, Malaysia, Indonesia and Thailand thrived in the 1980s and the 1990s as a result of prudent structural changes and selective industrial policy (Jomo and Chen 1997). Government intervention may not have been as significant a factor for economic growth; rather regional economic dynamics and direct foreign investment from the newly industrializing economies of the region have been cited as being far more critical in spurring development.

The impact of globalization driven by cross-border capital movements, rapid technology transfer, and communication and information flows has further heightened the momentum of economic growth in the region. On the international stage, it has been argued that the Asian economies might have gone 'too far in pursuing globalisation – and too fast' as the region has 'slipped into an over-reliance on external, extra-regional demand' (Lee 2009). Yet globalization has been touted as the major reason for jumps in household incomes and better living standards. In a nutshell, globalization has been instrumental in reducing poverty rates.

According to AT Kearney and Foreign Policy (AT Kearney 2007), Singapore and Hong Kong are the most globalized in economic terms among 72 countries in the world. Although Vietnam, which was included in the list in that year, did not make it to the top twenty, it was ranked tenth in terms of trade, indicating its commitment to trade liberalization. While globalization has been instrumental in the economic development of many countries in Asia, a mixture of positive and negative effects has been felt by different segments of the local populations. It has been argued that the economies of Southeast Asia have primarily been export-oriented and, therefore, have had the vigour to generate employment in the manufacturing sector (Rasiah and Yun 2009). Trade policies have also had an effect on women's employment and income (Fontana 2009). Export growth, facilitated by trade liberalization, does not mean, however, that the demand for female labour increased at a faster rate than demand for male labour, resulting in an equalization of women's and men's wages.

In reality, gender-based discrimination in labour markets has been found to persist in spite of economic liberalization (ibid.). Furthermore, a shift towards more capital- and skills-intensive forms of production and the relocation of jobs from the formal to the informal economy coupled with the removal of tariffs has reduced government revenues which has had a negative impact on women's employment (United Nations 2009). Thus, the assumption that globalization is effective in improving women's condition by creating manufacturing employment opportunities has been debunked as evidenced by the fact that gender wage gaps, for example, in the Asian region, have not closed.

Undoubtedly, rapid economic growth coupled with industrialization and globalization processes have provided Asian women with diverse employment opportunities (cf. Dunn and Skaggs 1999). This chapter aims to explore women's employment situation in Asia and the evidence for gender discrimination in employment by covering a number of related issues. While there have been greater numbers of women becoming active contributors to economic growth across the Asian region, the chapter shows how gender inequality persists because of structural, political, economic and social factors as reflected in the poor employment practices, worsening of labour conditions and lower wages for many women workers around the world as a result of globalization (cf. Prieto-Carrón 2008; Standing 1989, 1999; United Nations 2009). In particular, women have been marginalized in five respects: (1) the formal sector of the economy; (2) the gendered division of labour; (3) the exploitative nature of multinational corporations; (4) the double burden they face in balancing their roles as workers and caregivers in their families; and (5) the negative effects of structural adjustment programmes of the international financial institutions.

This chapter shows the extent to which Asian women are caught in a bind because their engagement in the labour market has mostly been regarded as complementary to the work men do and, thus, their work is accorded secondary economic value (Devasahayam and Yeoh 2007). By filling certain kinds of jobs assigned to them, whether in the countries of their home origin or across the countries in the region, they are unable to mitigate gender inequality and are forced to conceal and, in turn, reinforce, either consciously or unconsciously, the structural, social and cultural constructs that define their role and identity as women.

'Gainfully employed?' Asian women's experiences

The concept of labour force participation is useful because of its value in explaining why certain groups are employed in specific sectors. Specifically women's labour force participation rate refers to the ratio of their participation in the labour force in comparison to the total population. Labour force participation is generally determined by wage rates, changing attitudes to women taking up wage employment, women's educational level, delayed marriage, and low birthrates. Global indicators for women's employment which include status, sector and wage earnings may also be applied to Asian women, with men more likely than women to be employed in formal, salaried work, and with women more likely than men to be employed in flexible forms of labour and earn less for the same type of work.

Comparing the three major regions in Asia, namely Southeast Asia, South Asia and East Asia, South Asia is at one extreme of the spectrum with male economic participation rates more than twice that of female economic participation rates compared with East Asia where the gender gap is not as wide (see Figures 1.1 and 1.3). In both regions, nonetheless, there has been a steady rise in female economic participation in 1998–2008. In contrast, in Southeast Asia, women's economic participation has been fairly high although not as high as in East Asia; however, women's lagging rates of employment behind men's employment was slightly greater in 2008 as compared in 1998 (see Figure 1.2). Interestingly, women's economic participation levels have been much higher in Southeast Asia compared to South Asia.

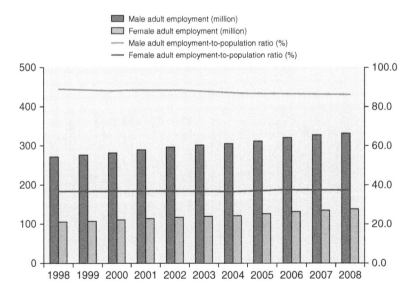

Figure 1.1 Male and female employment trends in South Asia, 1998–2008

Source: International Labour Organization (2009a).

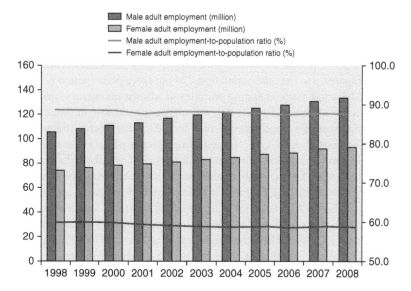

Figure 1.2 Male and female employment trends in Southeast Asia, 1998–2008

Source: International Labour Organization (2009a).

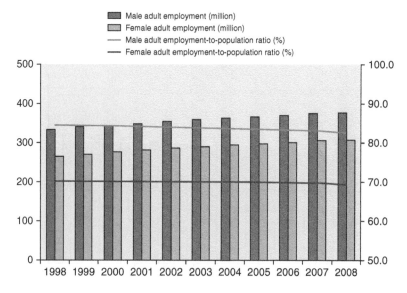

Figure 1.3 Male and female employment trends in East Asia, 1998–2008

Source: International Labour Organization (2009a)

East Asia in particular has been said to have a relatively small gender gap in terms of access to jobs as compared to the rest of Asia as well as other regions in the world (International Labour Organization 2009a). As such, the female vulnerable employment rate tends to be much lower there than in many parts of the world where women are often trapped in insecure employment characterized by low productivity and low earnings.

By and large, in the Asian region, female employment outnumbers male employment in some sectors in the developing countries. The export-oriented industries, for example, have been said to be a highly feminized sector. Since the 1980s, the economies of Asian countries have been heavily export-oriented (Radelet *et al.* 1997; Radelet and Sachs 1997; Sally 2008). This was found to be the case for Taiwan which was increasingly open to trade from the early 1980s to the early 1990s (Berik *et al.* 2002). These gains, however, have proven to be unsustainable in some economies because of shifts to skills- and capital-intensive forms of production which have favoured men over women (United Nations 2009). For example, in South Korea, employment rates for women declined from 39 to 35 per cent from 1980 to 2004 (Berik 2008). In contrast, the reverse was true of Thailand where there has been a steady rise in labour participation rates over the decades (Jomo 2009).

The persistence of gender

Nonetheless, there has been distinct gender segregation in most job sectors in many Asian countries. Women are over-represented in the electronics, textiles, and apparel sectors while men are found not to dominate any one employment sector (Berik *et al.* 2002). In fact, the greater the share of exports in the garment, textile and electronics industries, the greater the impact has been on the employment of women (Standing 1999).

It is not uncommon for patriarchal gender norms to have been found to govern hiring, training and labour policies and, as such, women tend to be excluded from higher-paid, skilled jobs compared with men. This was the argument made of South Korea and Taiwan (Cheng and Hsiung 1994; Nam 1994; Seguino 1997). In a survey, 94 per cent of women said that they faced greater obstacles securing full-time employment compared with men (Kang and Rowley 2005). Their conclusion is justifiable since 46 per cent of women are temporary workers, while only 15.2 per cent of women hold administrative and professional positions and 7 per cent are managers.

Taiwanese women, in contrast, have been found to fare better than their South Korean sisters. A study on female managers found that women of the current generation were more optimistic about securing promotions than the previous generation (Chou *et al.* 2005). In fact, women represent 19 per cent of managerial positions in Taiwan; this is a promising trend since women make up 41 per cent of the total workforce, reinforcing the idea that men make good managers while women play supportive roles even in the workplace.

With globalization, traditional gender ideologies have persisted. Describing the work carried out by men and women workers in the Fujitsu Electronics plant near Kagoshima, Custers (1997: 332) says:

> Cutting wafers is exclusively done by men, as is the maintenance of machines . . . Women in synthetic dresses stare through microscopes, checking whether the thin wires of the chips have been properly fixed to tiny plates. Why is this quality control exclusively done by women? The response is stereotype. One of the uniformed bosses told us: 'This work is very suitable for women, since they are used to doing stitching and embroidery. The work requires enormous concentration, and men are not fit for such monotonous labour.

Traditional gender ideologies continue at the transnational level. Migration has seen women take on jobs in the caregiving sector as nurses, caregivers and domestic workers in the more affluent labour-receiving countries faced with the care crisis (Beneria 2008; Ehrenreich and Hochschild 2003), a topic that will be taken up at greater length in Chapter 3. These jobs are considered to be typically female and are associated with the private sphere and, as such, there is the uncertainty around whether or not they constitute 'real' work (Oakley 1974). The act of feminizing these jobs has rendered them low paid, peripheral, insecure and less valued (United Nations 2004). The women who take on these jobs also risk not having social protection.

Where are the gender gaps?

It was once assumed that the gender gaps in the developed countries were not as wide as they were in the developing countries. A World Bank report of 1999 states:

> It is a fair generalization to say that the relative status of women is poor in the developing world, compared to developed countries. In the poorest countries, as a rule, girls get less education than boys, there is less investment in women's health than in men's, legal rights of women in the economy and in marriage are weaker than men's rights, and women have less political power.
>
> (Dollar and Gatti 1999: 20)

But this assumption has been contested (Khondker 2009). Ironically, countries with very high human development outcomes have shown lags in closing the gender gap (see Table 1.1). The impressive record of the Philippines makes this point. The Philippines, although it has a much lower overall human development profile, has done remarkably well in bridging the gender gap and has been placed in the top ten countries in the world, ahead of the Netherlands, Germany, Switzerland and the United States (World Economic Forum 2009). Compared with Singapore and other countries in the Asian region with more impressive economic growth

Table 1.1 Gender Gap Index in the Association of Southeast Asian Nation countries, 2009

Country	2009 Rank	Overall score	Economic participation and opportunity	Educational attainment
The Philippines	9	0.7579	0.7604	1.0000
Sri Lanka	16	0.7402	0.5734	0.9916
Thailand	59	0.6907	0.7216	0.9933
China	60	0.6907	0.6955	0.9797
Vietnam	71	0.6802	0.7349	0.8974
Japan	75	0.6769	0.6782	0.9851
Singapore	85	0.6664	0.6707	0.9370
Indonesia	93	0.6580	0.5722	0.9656
Bangladesh	94	0.6526	0.4552	0.9113
Brunei Darussalam	95	0.6524	0.6239	0.9923
Malaysia	101	0.6467	0.5653	0.9891
Cambodia	104	0.6410	0.6488	0.8568
Nepal	110	0.6213	0.4978	0.8164
India	114	0.6151	0.4125	0.8434
Korea, Republic	115	0.6146	0.5204	0.8936
Pakistan	132	0.4609	0.2334	0.6147

Source: Adapted from World Economic Forum (2009).

records, the Philippines has the highest number of women in legislative and managerial positions. Singapore, in contrast, has been found to be lagging behind although the proportion of female managers is relatively high, in excess of 25 per cent (Benson and Yukongdi 2005).

Other examples are Thailand, China and Vietnam, countries that are clearly not in the developed nation cluster and yet have had fairly high rates of economic participation for women compared with Japan and Singapore. In spite of the fairly high rates for economic participation for Vietnam, this is not to say that the rates have been consistently high for these countries; it has been shown that rates have dropped from 92 per cent in 1997 to 86 per cent in 2005 as a result of gender discriminatory practices in the private sector (Chaudhuri 2010; Liu 2004).

Does education matter?

Much has been said about the role of education in securing women a footing in the workplace and improving their options in the labour markets. Education has been found to be a significant factor for women's economic participation (United Nations 2009). In a study of eight Southeast Asian and South Asian countries, not only was female education higher in Vietnam than all the other countries, but economic participation rates were also the highest (Chaudhuri 2010). The case of the Philippines also attests to this point. But closing the gender gap on education has not been the trend in all the Asian countries (see Table 1.1).

Barriers to achieving parity in education among boys and girls include the lack of suitable sanitation for girls; school fees which make parents prioritize sending boys instead of girls; distance from the home to school and the safety in travelling long distances to school; and the practice of early marriage (World Economic Forum 2009). For example, Thailand shows great strides in closing the education gap between the sexes but in terms of economic participation, it appears to fall short of Vietnam in spite of the latter's labour force participation for women being lower than for men. In fact, based on data from the Global Gender Gap Report 2009 (see Table 1.1), education levels were high for women in Malaysia and Brunei Darussalam and yet economic participation rates were much lower than expected. It must be noted, however, that although economic participation rates are fairly low for Brunei Darussalam, it has managed to move up in its rankings owing to improvements in labour force participation (World Economic Forum 2009). Nonetheless in these two countries, Islamic teachings regarding male superiority and the segregation of the sexes in all areas of life may have been a contributing factor.

This context has shaped not only the employment choices women have made and their perceived potential for promotion in the workplace, but whether or not to engage in wage work in spite of having received an education. The same argument may be applied to the case of Bangladesh where it was found that women filled only 5.1 per cent of administrative and managerial positions and 6 per cent of government jobs (Zafarullah 2000). In fact, the converse is also true where low educational levels among women demonstrate their low economic participation. In Asia, Pakistan demonstrates this trend.

A caveat in this regard, however, must be made. Although education increases the employment opportunities and options for women, there continues to be a gender bias in some subjects and, therefore, women are concentrated in some professions while others have become more male-dominated. Data from Singapore illustrates this point. Although there were women taking up study in all the different subjects, there were larger proportions of women in certain fields such as education (72 per cent), humanities and social sciences (64 per cent), health sciences (59 per cent), and the fine and applied arts (58 per cent). Men, in contrast, were concentrated in the Engineering Sciences (83 per cent) and Information Technology (65 per cent) (see Figure 1.4). It is interesting to note that these trends parallel traditional divisions in the West.

While education may open up career options, there are instances in which sex discrimination continues to exist, thereby blocking women from taking on wage work commensurate to their educational achievements. Brinton and Lee (2001) have given the example of Japan and South Korea where highly educated women have been deliberately excluded from white labour markets although the trend was found to reverse in Japan when the demand for educated workers exceeded the supply provided by male graduates. The response to such a situation has left some educated women workers as 'discouraged workers', as in the case of South Korean women (ibid.: 136). Standing (1976, as cited in Brinton and Lee 2001) mentions how it is not surprising if these women choose to retreat from the labour force completely rather than take on low-paid and low-status jobs.

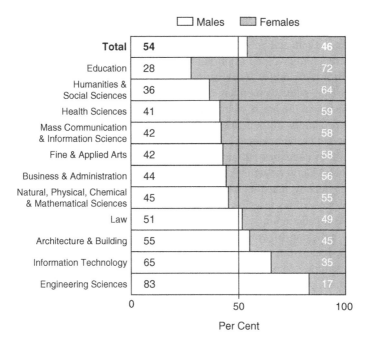

Figure 1.4 Resident student graduates by field of study and sex, 2005

Source: Ang (2006).

The persistent challenges of the working Asian woman

Becoming increasingly engaged in wage work does not mean that women do not face obstacles. Technological changes in industrial sectors have been found to impact negatively on women's employment. As a result of technological restructuring, men are able to preserve their high-paying jobs while women are excluded from competing for such jobs. In East Asia, Berik *et al.* (2002) say that technological changes also mean greater job losses for women. Primarily women are not able to compete for such jobs because of the lack of technological training from which they might have been excluded. As such, when industries undergo technological changes, job competition intensifies and, in turn, the gender wage gap widens as women are not able to secure the higher-paid jobs.

Furthermore, women felt the discriminatory effects of downsizing more than men as a result of structural changes in industries because they tend to have less education and work experience (Berik and Rodgers 2008). In China and Vietnam, data on women retrenched from government positions showed that many face great difficulties in securing other work and tend instead to enter the informal sector (Appleton *et al.* 2002; Rama 2002).

Although a lack of constraints to restrict women from engaging in wage work in most of Asia is the case, social norms expect that they continue to keep up their primary role as caregivers in spite of working. In this case, women are expected to balance the worker and caregiver roles. The pattern was consistent in much of Asia (Devasahayam and Yeoh 2007; Hirao 2001; Yu 2001). But because of gender ideologies regarding women's familial responsibilities, this has a direct bearing on the choice for the kinds of wage work they take on (United Nations 2009). This is not surprising since women have been found to put in greater number of hours of unpaid work in the home when there was a young child in the home. Because of these expectations of their roles in the family, some women sought to put their families first over their careers.

In a study of decisions on family size in Malaysia, Devasahayam (2004) discovered that Malay women would choose to prioritize raising a family more than career, feeling that they cannot afford to postpone motherhood compared to the prospects of securing wage work. Interestingly The Global Gender Gap Report (World Economic Forum 2009) raises the concept of the 'motherhood gap', referring to women's decision to work. For the cohort sample comprised of women from ages 35–44, women from the Philippines, together with Chile, Argentina, Mexico, Colombia, Ecuador, Austria and Hungary, with three children or more were less likely to work compared with women with no children.

Wage gaps: the persistent gender gap

The asymmetrical relationship between men and women in the labour market is evident in work opportunities, experiences, rewards and challenges. While paid work may be taken as an indicator of women's progress (Clark *et al.* 1991; Young *et al.* 1996), there persists a gender gap evidenced in men earning more than women, holding higher management positions than women, dominating the more lucrative jobs, and having greater access to work in the formal sector. Generally, the factors for the persistence of the gender gap are related to employment and earnings opportunities and to the opportunity costs of not working. Thus, the trends in Asia are no different from the rest of the world. Globally, it has been estimated that women earn 16.5 per cent less than men (International Trade Union Confederation 2008). In the region, Brunei Darussalam, India, Pakistan and Sri Lanka have been found to have the widest gender wage gaps while Hong Kong, China has the smallest, according to 2008 estimates (OECD/KOREA Policy Centre 2009).

Since the late 1980s, Japan, South Korea and Taiwan have enjoyed great economic growth and rising income levels. But men and women have not shared in the economic prosperity equally. The gender gap is most pronounced in earnings. Based on the 2006 EASS data, a study found that the wage gap between the sexes was highest in Korea, followed by Japan (Chang 2009). By contrast, Taiwan had the most positive picture with women earning close to 82 per cent of what men earned. It is difficult to surmise what the factors are for the discrepancy since Japan was the first to industrialize, followed by Taiwan and lastly South Korea, although Brinton (2001) attempts to present some causes on the labour demand side, namely firm size, size of the public sector, and the demand for educated workers. But generally, there continues to be a wage gap among women in South Korea and Taiwan because they are excluded from higher-paid jobs (Cheng and Hsiung 1994; Nam 1994; Seguino 1997).

It was found that Taiwanese and South Korean women in the same industry and doing the same jobs as men were paid less: in short, they were not receiving 'equal pay for work of equal value' (Berik *et al.* 2002: 10).

Southeast Asia also demonstrates significant wage gaps between men and women. According to the Global Gender Gap Report (World Economic Forum 2009), the gender wage gap differs markedly in the Southeast Asian countries. In terms of wage equality for similar work, Singapore's score (0.79) was above the sample average (0.66) and ranked 9 out of 191 countries. Thailand also scored fairly well with its ranking of 17 for wage equality. But for Indonesia and Malaysia, their rankings were 31 and 36 respectively. It appears that the level of development does not bear on the gender wage gap as Iceland and Finland scored 50 and 47 respectively for wage equality in spite of being ranked first and second in the study for overall performance.

As in measures for women's empowerment in terms of labour force employment, there does not appear to be a strong link between the level of economic development of a country and male–female wage ratios (OECD/KOREA Policy Centre 2009). But this may be the case when contrasting occupations across sectors rather than within sectors since it has been shown that the gender wage gap appears to decrease with increasing economic development within narrowly defined occupations (Oostendorp 2009). Based on International Labour Organization 2008 statistics (as cited in OECD/KOREA Policy Centre 2009), wage differentials between men and women were much wider in Japan and South Korea than they were in Bangladesh and Thailand, countries at a lower economic development stage. In contrast to Japan and South Korea, Hong Kong and Singapore have demonstrated lower wage differentials between the sexes.

But taking longitudinal rates into account in terms of female to male earned income, the Asian region shows a mixed picture with some countries showing declines while others increases. According to the UNDP 2008 Human Development Report (as cited in OECD/KOREA Policy Centre 2009), out of 20 countries in the Asian and Pacific region, women in seven countries (namely Brunei Darussalam, India, Indonesia, Laos, Myanmar, Nepal and Sri Lanka) are worse off as the gender wage gap has widened in the past ten years. Among countries where the gender wage gap has shrunk, Hong Kong in China has seen the greatest improvement; the gender wage gap in this case has halved. Other countries that have shown a drop in the ratio of female earned income to male earned income are South Korea, Singapore and the Philippines, although the drop has been modest.

Berik *et al.* (2002), citing a number of studies, affirm that export competitiveness dampens women's wages and reinforces wage inequalities between the sexes. Women's wages in these countries are suppressed because many enter home-based work, promoted by state policies that limit their bargaining power. Others have argued that it is the low wages accorded to women that have in fact spurred foreign investment by lowering labour unit costs and in turn women bearing the burden of wage inequality at the expense of economic growth (Seguino 2000).

Evidently gender-based occupational and industrial segregation mediate the wage rates between the sexes. In a study on Bangladesh commissioned by the International Labour Organization, it was found that in spite of controlling for differences in age, education, industry, occupational type and location, women still earned 15.9 per cent less than men. This is apart from the fact that women were concentrated in lower-paid jobs and did not have access to the kinds of jobs dominated by men (International Labour Organization 2009a). The largest wage gaps were found in the construction, hotel and restaurant industries and interestingly the smallest wage gaps were found in the health, education and social work sectors – fields dominated by women.

Many reasons have been put forward to explain the gender wage gap. Undoubtedly education and relevant skills play a critical role in determining the wages of men and women. Because women are less likely to receive a college education, they tended to earn less than men. This was the case of Japan and South Korea (Chang 2009). Taiwan's data shows a sharp contrast. Because more women have tertiary education compared with men, the earnings gap was not as wide as the Japanese and South Korean examples. But it has also been pointed out that with greater participation in the global economy, firms are more likely to engage in 'cost-cutting practices that may affect female employees differently than male employees, particularly if sex discrimination plays a role in firms' hiring and pay decisions' (Berik *et al.* 2002: 1). The same was found of the Bangladeshi case where education was a determining factor in closing the wage gap. Completing secondary education enables a woman to earn 4 per cent less than her male counterpart while a woman who has only a primary education would end up earning as much as 22 per cent less than her male counterpart (International Labour Organization 2009a).

The widening of the wage gap between the sexes has been occurring in some countries. Zveglich and Rodgers (2004) have attempted to explain the growing gender wage gap in Taiwan over the past two decades. That employers seek out workers with 'potential experience rather than actual experience', they argue, might have 'masked a growing gender gap in total labor market experience' (ibid.: 865). In this regard, women may be automatically disqualified since they would have had to exit the workforce to provide care for their children. In this sense, 'they have less actual work experience for each year of potential experience' (ibid.: 865). Another factor cited was Taiwan's integration into the global economy where competition among firms and industries has led to cost-cutting. Women have had to bear the brunt because of their weak bargaining power especially when there is a 'shift in traditionally female-intensive production activities offshore', leaving female workers with little choice but to accept lower wages (ibid.: 867). Thus in countries heavily linked to global markets like Taiwan, 'keeping the cost of labor low has encouraged the growth of demand for female labor' (Moghadam 1999: 370; see also United Nations 2009). Conversely, should labour costs provided by women go up, this would work against them since they are less likely to be employed.

Conclusion

Globalization has brought an economic boom in the lives of Asian women. But globalization has been a double-edged sword for women: while pushing them into the labour force, on the one hand, it has led to a process of 'female proletarianization' on the other (Moghadam 1999: 372). Asian women are negatively affected by trade liberalization especially if they engage in wage work in sectors exposed to import competition. Moreover, the greater the openness of the country to export competitiveness, the greater the negative impact this has on the gender gap. This negative effect women workers experience becomes compounded if opportunities to find employment in other sectors become 'limited due to lack of assets, employers' prejudices and other market biases' (Fontana 2009: 3). On the downside, taking on jobs with less security and lower wages is more likely to lead to poverty, especially in the face of declining household budgets as a result of rising costs of living (Moghadam 1999).

Governments have to face the fact that they have to pay a hefty price for the gender gap in employment. It has been found that the cost of gender inequality for national economies is fairly considerable. Based on data gathered from a number of Asian economies, the Economic and Social Commission for Asia and the Pacific found that the gender gap in labour force participation costs some $42–47 billion to the countries concerned (United Nations Economic and Social Commission for Asia and the Pacific 2007). Closing the gap, thus, benefits them as much as women. But whether they will act on the issue would largely depend if they see the gender gap in employment to be critical to sustaining their economies.

Some Asian governments have committed themselves to remove differing types of discrimination against women. There has been experimentation with legislation to prevent sex discrimination against women from securing wage work. In Taiwan, the Labor Standards Law enacted in 1984 prohibits gender discrimination among employers. Japan and Taiwan have similar legal mechanism to protect women (Zveglich and Rodgers 2004). Japan also has a Gender Equality Law to focus on equal opportunity in economic participation. But as in any other legislation, enforcement is an issue. Often these laws are not accompanied by relevant policy initiatives and budgetary resources to ensure gender equality. For example, while the Philippine government has set aside 5 per cent of its national budget for women, Singapore has no such initiative (UNIFEM 2005).

In an increasingly globalized world, thus, women have had not only to confront rapid economic development but semblances of gender inequality. In some countries, the inequalities faced by women have led to the emergence of a broad array of women's organizations, whether as members of unions or critics of trade liberalization in transnational feminist networks. These women, at the transnational and national levels, have 'rais[ed] questions about social and gender arrangements and making demands on employers, governments, and international financial institutions' (Moghadam 1999: 386). Clearly women are not patiently enduring the unequal situations which they face. In this regard, women are not aiming for an 'Asia that has undergone development and destruction created on male principles such as domination, competition, efficiency, plundering and homogenization, but . . .' as Matsui (1999: 186) asserts, 'an Asia characterized by symbiosis and human rights based on feminine principles such as self-reliance, solidarity, caring, sharing and diversity.'

2 Changing patterns of caregiving and emotional labour in Asia

Theresa Devasahayam and Ann Brooks

Introduction

Changes in population structure have been recorded worldwide. In particular, family size has been shrinking with the increasing numbers of women absorbed into the labour force (Caldwell and Caldwell 2005; Ogawa *et al.* 2005). Demographic trends in Asia have not shown any deviation (Haughton 1997; Hull 1994; Prachuabmoh and Mithranon 2003; Robey 1989; Yap 2002). The dual-income couple has become the norm rather than the exception owing to increasing levels of education among women and the need to engage in wage work as a state and domestic imperative. In spite of the changing demographic patterns, the organization of caring and parenting has undergone some but not significant transformation. The social injunction is that women are the primary caregivers and caretakers in the family, while men are perceived as the main breadwinners.

The experiences and the ideas on mothering and caregiving among different groups of women across Asia have been different. This chapter focuses on gender ideologies that shape the lives of Asian working women. Specifically it explores the indigenous and other ideologies around caregiving characteristic to the region. Unlike the Western context, care work is intimately bound up with cultural notions of the dutiful woman/wife. Indigenous ideologies have to be combined with state ideologies which emphasize the need for women to combine caregiving with being economically productive.

Working women in Asia are caught in a bind as workers and caregivers. Like women in the West, the act of balancing the worker and caregiver roles is fraught with tensions (see Chapter 5; Becker and Moen 1999; Blair-Loy 2003; Rhode 1997; Williams 2000). Because of the unequal allocation of care work in the family, women's potential to be empowered through wage work has had ambivalent outcomes. An obvious implication of the unequal allocation of housework on women is that they are not able to fully concentrate on workplace demands.

Women are, in addition, constantly bombarded by conflicting messages. Aside from cultural and social norms mandating women's commitment to their caregiver role, the economic growth policies of many countries in the region require women to work. Women, however, face constraints while engaging in wage work and, consequently, many have found themselves being forced onto the fringes of the labour force. Many other professional women are in the upper echelons of the labour market with significant corporate demands made on them (Brooks 2006).

Some theorists have been optimistic, suggesting that women find ways to combine the experiences, roles, and responsibilities of work and family (Garey 1999). This is especially true in Southeast Asia where women have been presented with options to balance family commitments and work demands by relying on relatives or hiring the domestic labour of other women (see Chapters 3, 4 and 6 in this volume). As such, the coping strategies employed among Asian women differ from women in the Western hemisphere (see Chapter 5 in this volume).

Women in Southeast Asia, as in other regions, do not form a unified, undifferentiated category. The experiences of working-class women are markedly different from those of middle-class women. They face greater tensions having to cope with wage work as well as provide care for their families because their options compared with their middle-class counterparts tend to be far more limited. We are interested in exploring the experiences of both groups across Asia.

Asia, ideologies and emotion work

In Southeast Asia, gender ideologies are heavily bound up with how the identities of men and women are constructed. Despite social, cultural and demographic changes in the region (see Brooks 2010), women are still largely responsible for emotion work (Ruddick 1998). As shown earlier, such work requires both physical and emotional labour. Because caring for family members is emotion work for which only women are responsible, as such, they are unable to extricate themselves from this role. As such for them, any activity, even those outside the home, impinges dramatically on how they assume their role in the home. While men are increasingly involved in emotion work in the family, they still tend to be seen as primarily the breadwinner. This is particularly true among working-class households in Asia.

In Indonesia, as in other places, Sullivan (1994) speaks of how cultural notions of gender function to help keep Javanese men and women in socially desirable places. In a neighbourhood in Java she studied, Sullivan noted a clear demarcation of roles: men are providers and protectors of their families and representatives of their families to the rest of society, while women are confined to being charged with managing the activities of the home. These gender notions of the male and female roles in the household are reinforced by local definitions of the hearthhold (*somahan*) and household (*rumah tangga*). While *somahan* is viewed as the locus of food preparation, the domain of women, *rumah tangga*, which is the formal and taxable unit recognized by the government, is perceived as the domain of men.

Among the Javanese,

> This segregation is not seen as a means by which men gain access to, and monopolise power in, formal structures and processes. Rather, it is acknowledged as a rational way to organise society according to the 'natural' roles each gender plays in the process of human reproduction . . . these 'natural' roles and task allocations are perceived, at another level, as unified and mutually

supportive, because they are oriented towards the same objective: secure and harmonious family life. [And] on these grounds it is held that women and men enjoy equal social status.

(ibid.: 111–12)

That the roles of men and women are clearly demarcated in Southeast Asia is a point well articulated by Karim (1995: 36):

Numerous Southeast Asian cultures allow both men and women to explore their sexual differences freely, without inhibition and without shifting the natural attributes which both sexes have to offer one another – women as 'feminine' and sexually accommodating, as mothers, home-makers, food processors and keepers of communal and ritual relations; men as 'masculine' and sexually aggressive, as fathers, hunters, economic providers and guardians of political and religious institutions.

From the perspective of Asian governments, gender is not seen as a marker of stratification and hierarchy, 'male' and 'female' are equal but different, with each performing complementary roles. Women's tolerance is, of course, changing dramatically in relation to this rhetoric particularly in the cities and urban areas. However, attitudes in rural areas are still underpinned by convention.

Discourses of gender in the region map out women's primary identities to be that of wives and mothers, a pattern discovered by Stivens (1996) in her research in Rembau, Negeri Sembilan (Malaysia). The cultural expectations of parenting demanded of them are never looked upon with negative feelings; instead as she (ibid.: 183) says: 'women articulated clearly maternalist ideas that childcare was infinitely enjoyable, rewarding and fulfilling'. Children were coddled constantly and never left to cry. As years went on, they were disciplined but with very little corporeal punishment involved. In later years, however, girls begin to learn the roles of a woman: they helped to play the caregiver role to their younger siblings and some household tasks. In Langkawi, in Malaysia, the same pattern of childrearing was found. While it is not uncommon for grandparents' or parents' siblings to become engaged in parenting, the mother, however, is thought to be the most suitable nurturer (Carsten 1997). The matrifocal character of some societies in insular Southeast Asia means that emotional ties are strong between children (especially daughters) and mothers. By contrast, the relationship between sons and fathers tends to be 'formal, [and by extension marked by] . . . avoidance . . . although fathers are treated with respect', a pattern Alexander and Alexander (2001) discovered among the Javanese.

Emotional ties are built through sharing of food. In fact, integral to parenting by Southeast Asian women is the offering and acceptance of food. For Malays living on the island of Langkawi, Carsten (1997) maintains that while kinship may be thought to be acquired at birth, this is actualized through the sharing of bodily fluids through breastfeeding between a woman and her child. It is this sharing of milk which at a later stage becomes the sharing of meals to produce kinship. In Carsten's (ibid.: 127) own words:

Milk, then, may be understood as the enabling substance of kinship: a source of emotional and physical connectedness . . . To a lesser degree, food cooked on the natal hearth has the same qualities. A tiny infant may be given water cooked in the *dapur* as a substitute for its mother's milk. Food becomes blood. And through the day-to-day sharing of meals cooked in the same hearth, those who live together in one house come to have substance in common.

It is not surprising then that the activity of cooking is bound up with women's parenting qualities; thus, cooking is viewed as a tool through which they express and reinforce their role in the family (Devasahayam 2001).

In this context it could be argued that women do not see themselves to be blindly embracing a gender ideology that places them in a hegemonic relationship with men. Instead this perception toward nurturing through food sharing is indicative of a specific cultural orientation emphasizing the activity to be of prime value to them. To put it differently, nurturing through cooking is a cultural value that is vigorously upheld among Southeast Asian women because they see this activity not as a burden but rather as a positive experience related to their gendered identity.

An anthropological view of the association of cooking and gendered identity can be seen in the following case. Because only women undertake cooking as an extension of their nurturing role, cultural notions associate the kitchen (Malay; *dapur*) with women and, hence, there is the phrase: '*tempat orang perempuan selalu di dapur*' (lit. the place of a woman is always in the kitchen), commonly used to describe Malay women (Devasahayam 2001). Moreover, the association of the kitchen with women is strengthened by the fact that men are absent from the house for a substantial part of the day (Carsten 1995). This notion also holds true for the working woman because cooking and serving food is her prerogative (Hing *et al.* 1984). Malay women, however, are not the only ones to cook; this activity is also carried out by men but only in a ritual context such as the *kenduri* (feast) (Devasahayam 2001). In fact at feasts, men dominate in special cooking with women playing the supportive role. But when men cook, this kind of cooking is tied up with their professional role and not their gendered status.

Even if women have taken on jobs abroad and are absent from the household temporarily, they still carry the distinction of the parental roles. In a study of transnational working mothers, Salazar Parreñas (2005) found that Filipina women continue to shoulder the burden of providing care across thousands of miles. In doing so, they 'resist gender ambiguity and conform to gender boundaries' (ibid.: 7). Here, transnational working women continue to reinforce the separate and complementary roles of the sexes which in turn are the social expectations placed on non-migrating women as well. Although they may be contributing financially toward their children, this is never regarded to be part of the caregiver role of women; instead it is a firmly held idea by their children that the role of breadwinner is always that of the father in the family. Here the commonly held notion is that the income a working woman generates does not displace the breadwinner role of the father and that she works only to facilitate her husband's role.

Thus, in some parts of Southeast Asia, gendered roles are still the predominant models. Luong (2003: 209) documents the 'double bind' Vietnamese women encounter: while being presented with increasing economic and employment opportunities, at the same time they are constrained by the continued practice of patrilocal coresidence expected of young couples, which he says contributes to

> [T]he persistence of domestic labor division and . . . [the] emphasis on women's economic contributions simply as part of their *domestic* duties, which in turn exert[s] a major adverse impact on women's abilities to participate on an equal footing with men in the political arena.

In the agricultural areas in the north of Vietnam, wives bear the greatest load in carrying out the different tasks in agricultural production, while men played the major role in decision-making (Thi 1996). Asymmetries in gender are fast changing among the more educated as well as the urban elites. Brooks (2010) shows how younger Vietnamese women in urban Vietnam are rejecting traditional patterns of marriage for singlehood and better paid jobs. The distinction between urban and rural patterns of life in Vietnam, Thailand and countries in Southeast Asia are presenting new models for women and men.

Work–life balance in an Asian context

Balancing the demands of work, career and home raises challenges for women globally. Women in Asia face unique structural and social pressures to maintain both roles so that they do not neglect their caregiver role for their worker role. Many women in Asia are expected to strive towards exerting equal vigour in each of these spheres of life but the result for many is that the balancing act presents multiple burdens to them.

Messages upholding 'traditional values' have led to conflicts in women's attempt to balance the worker and mother roles. Contemporary women in Malaysia and Singapore are increasingly bombarded by messages reinstating their mother role from different quarters. The state has been pronouncing judgements on women's place in society through its various policies; corporations have had their share of pushing work–life balance initiatives; and simultaneously there is anxiety over the impending moral decline and family values from religious groups. Contradictions in the lives of working women abound. If the work–life balance approach is the solution to help working women cope with their work and family roles, certainly only a segment is privileged: mainly the professional women and other white-collar job holders. The received models, according to Stivens (2007), do nothing for the working-class women, rural women and others on the periphery.

The confluence of these factors has left many women 'exhausted and stressed out [and] . . . responding in some cases by having fewer children, or by delaying child-birth and finding that this has robbed them of motherhood, or by foregoing marriage and children all together' (ibid.: 42). This is not surprising since women undertake the bulk of the caring work in the family. Furthermore, women are expected to be competent in their execution of the mother role in spite of working. Stivens points out that this is evidenced particularly in how men are left out of the discourses on family and fertility.

The impact of structural forces on women's lives has also been felt in other countries. Because of the declining fertility rate in contemporary Japan, the ideal of 'good mothering' has been reiterated by various institutions. The balancing act becomes especially problematic when women are expected to produce 'high quality' children in their role as caregivers (Hirao 2007: 54). This has resulted in women feeling pulled in different directions, setting the trend for many younger women to abandon the idea of becoming mothers themselves. While the Japanese government has conscientiously installed comprehensive and supportive structures to help women reconcile work-and-family conflicts, these have been said to be largely ineffective because of the persistent demands of the labour market on women's workforce participation and the unchanging social norms regarding gender roles in the family. The contradiction in Japanese policies is nonetheless also responsible for the difficulties for women trying to balance the worker and caregiver roles. On the one hand, there are policies that appear to assist women in the balancing act while, on the other, the restructured school system overburdens women because they are expected to take on the role of educational agents for their children in the family.

Singapore, like Japan, is also under threat with falling fertility rates and institutional forces have been equally forceful in reinforcing women's gendered roles. For many decades, the Singapore government has adopted proactive measures to encourage women to engage in wage work. But state policies are equally contradictory as, on the one hand, women are encouraged into the workforce and to be efficient workers while, on the other, they have been coaxed not to abandon the mother role. This contradiction is clearly captured in state constructions of motherhood and mothering presented to its citizenry by way of Singapore's family law, particularly in the context of custody battles over children.

While family law acknowledges the importance of both the mother and father roles in providing care for children, Ong (2007) notes that the law primarily views the mother as the primary caregiver, especially should the children be young, while the father is regarded as the natural breadwinner (see also Lee 2011). How maintenance is decided clearly demonstrates the distinction in gender roles as well. In a custody battle, often fathers end up paying for the maintenance of the child(ren). This occurs even should the children be given into the care of the mother. Interestingly, in cases of fathers who gain custody, mothers are exempted from the same role or if they do pay maintenance, the sum is often much lower than that which the father would have to pay.

While the law reinforces gender in the above cited contexts, there is another instance in which gender is not only asserted but women are disadvantaged. Ong (2007) found that working women who spend less time with their children because of workplace demands are at risk of losing custody of their children. In fact, in a custody battle, if a mother has been shown to have slackened in her role as caregiver and if the father is able to prove his fervour in providing care for the children, the courts end up favouring the father. In effect, a working mother who is seeking a divorce is in a precarious position. She needs to demonstrate that in spite of engaging in wage work, she has had no difficulties in providing for her children's needs and, in fact, has not allowed her work demands to interfere with her family role.

For some women, retreating completely from the workforce owing to practical and emotional issues is the most viable coping mechanism. Based on interviews with women who had left the workforce to care for their families, Lai and Huang (2004) discovered that it was not the heavy demands at the workplace or the burden of playing the primary role as caregiver that determined women's decision to opt for full-time motherhood, but rather the decision that they were the best individuals to meet the interests of their children. The women with whom they spoke, however, divulged that their husbands' heavy work schedules were critical in pushing them to make their decision to leave wage employment. Principally, they felt that if the father was too busy and was engulfed by work, the mother should not find herself in a similar position but rather devote her attention, time and energy to her children.

Clearly, women's decision for non-work in this case was impelled by the fact that their husbands' jobs were more important than theirs and that it was acceptable for men to have fast-track careers while women were forced to see their own career aspirations as inconsequential. But while faced with 'angst and ambivalence over giving up paid work' (ibid.: 99), simultaneously women recognized their inadequacy 'to strike an effective balance between family and work' (ibid.: 108). Women were thus forced to leave the workforce because of their inability to balance careers and caring for the children.

Young educated women may also scale back on work because of the need to start a family. Narratives gathered from tertiary-educated Malay women in Malaysia on fertility decisions reveal that they are more likely to choose to scale back on paid work, and prioritize having a family earlier on in their childbearing lives (Devasahayam 2004). And when asked about family life, they spoke of putting family first above career, although not necessarily in sacrificial terms. Hence, shelving career goals is not seen as unusual.

However Jones (2003, 2004), in evidence from Southeast Asia, shows a distinct demographic pattern of delayed marriage, singlehood and decisions not to have children at all in order to address the career imperative (see also Brooks 2010).

While motherhood demands have been the reason for why some working women are forced to scale back from the workplace, others have had to forego the time they could have spent on rest, community activities, and self-development, should they have chosen not to allow their careers to be affected (Yarr 1996). Particularly in Vietnam where women engage in political activities on an equal footing with men, working women face pressures in completing household chores because of the limited time they have as a consequence of working. For them, not being able to engage in community activities is tantamount to being silenced, as they will not be able to voice their interests to government officials.

Engagement in the labour force, nonetheless, is seen to be personally satisfying for a growing number of women in the region, although they are fully conscious of the struggles that lie ahead if they choose to be a working mother. Filipino women have been found to see employment as a significant variable contributing to their intellectual, social, economic, emotional, spiritual and moral development (Pedrajas 1997). This was the experience of especially middle-class women. They were more concerned about applying their education and training, exercising their interest in a particular job, and engaging in self-development. Working-class women had a different story to tell. Engagement in the labour force for them was an extension of their traditional homemaker role. The working-class woman felt a greater urgency to work to play the co-provider role with her husband in order to meet the financial needs of the family. While recognizing that their own employment had favourable consequences on their own children, both middle- and working-class women are aware that working meant that the time spent with their children would be reduced considerably. Thus, there remains a strong class dimension to assessments towards career and family for women in Southeast Asia.

State policies and the media

That state policies influence women's participation in the labour force is a consistent trend in Southeast Asia. Women are constantly encouraged by state discourses to become equal players in the growth of their country's economies, while at the same time they are continuously being reminded that they should never give up their primary calling as caregivers in the family (Lee *et al.* 1999). Singapore is an exemplary case. Scholars have argued that state policies have been blatantly patriarchal, consistently portraying women as mothers, wives and daughters-in-law as their primary identities and, in turn, 'managers of the private sphere' who are responsible for reproduction and tending to the needs of the family, while men are regarded as soldiers entrusted with the more masculine and public roles (Chew 2004; Chew and Singam 2004; Kong and Chan 2000; Lazar 1999).

While the Singapore state has assertively through policy and campaigns made its impressions of women known, according to one interpretation, the power the state has wielded on its citizenry has not been as strong as it is made out to be (Teo 2009). Thus, while the state has its own 'ideas' about how gender should be played out in the family, in reality, it has been perceived to have 'limited agency' (ibid.: 550).

In the initial years of women's engagement in the labour force, Malaysian working women were seen to be 'bad mothers', if they failed to live up to their primary caregiver role and instead chose to press on to develop their careers. The discourse on mothering and working has changed in the more recent decades, as women were regarded as the 'new middle-class jugglers' of the work–life balance. As pointed out by Stivens (2007), at the heart of this concept is the idea that this can only reinforce gendered views further, since work–life balance initiatives have mostly been targeted at working women rather than working men, thereby reinforcing the stereotype that women are the principal caregivers. But Malaysian women are not merely 'exploring a number of options in combining work and motherhood, there is growing evidence that these identities as "mother" and "worker" may well be increasingly mutually constitutive, in complex configurations' (ibid.: 34). To this end, each identity is bound up with the other and, in postmodern Malaysia, the concept of 'working mother' cannot be divorced from the twin concepts of 'modernity' and 'tradition' and, as Stivens notes, the modern woman is synonymous with the working woman.

Among Indonesian women with an upper secondary or tertiary education, labour force participation is high and rising (Jones 2002). Since women wield considerable bargaining power as they are well placed with good job prospects ahead of them, many enter the labour force. While Javanese urban women have been found to openly embrace the Western concept of 'career wife' and 'professional women' with ease as it supports middle-class women's aspirations for a career, they expect to juggle the two roles of worker and wife/mother. Evidence is rife that the Indonesian state has been desperately urging women to think and act accordingly as good citizens, and by this they mean adopting family planning practices to control the country's population. But it is also state ideology that constantly reminds them not to lose sight of their primary role as caregiver.

The official ideology of women's and men's roles is propagated through two channels: the Family Welfare Development Program and the Indonesian family welfare movement which bears the acronym PKK (Sullivan 1994). State ideologies reaffirm local ideologies of gender by asserting that men's and women's roles are different and yet complementary. Definitions of the distinctive roles of men and women took on full force during the New Order Period (Robinson and Bessell 2002: 3):

> Men and women had clearly defined roles that reinforced particular constructions of identity. Importantly, the public and private spheres were clearly – and artificially – separated, with women's roles confined largely to the private sphere. The ideal New Order woman was a mother, wife and household manager. This ideology has been captured by the term 'state ibuism'.

Thus, while state policies have urged women to actively contribute to the country's modernization and development processes, this, however, does not divest them of their main duties: to be supportive of their husbands and to perform their rightful roles as mothers. On this, Alexander and Alexander (2001) have found that if Javanese women managed their own business enterprises, they would speak of their efforts as *rewange bapake* (helping father), suggesting that men are the main breadwinners while their contributions were only supplementary to their husbands' income.

Singlehood and caregiving

One would expect that the unmarried woman does not face the pressures of her married sisters, but they too have to undertake the caregiver role, although not to children or husbands but rather to elderly parents. Unmarried women, unlike unmarried men (and to some extent married women), are often left to provide care for ageing parents. In a cross-country study on ageing populations across the Asia and Pacific region (Mujahid 2006), it is recorded that although traditionally the male offspring bears the responsibility of providing care for his parents, the reality shows that the daughter-in-law or daughter are more likely to provide care or otherwise supervise paid help on the day-to-day level to provide economic support to ageing relatives.

Unmarried women frequently do find themselves thrust into the role of elder caregiver by their own married siblings who insist that the role should be shared. Singaporean unmarried women have reported that their own married siblings under the pretext of having their own children to care for have insisted that the unmarried sibling(s) take on the eldercare responsibility (Devasahayam 2003a). Among unmarried women who work, the anxieties of balancing the caregiver and the worker roles are also a reality. The management of the two spheres of their lives is more critical especially since these women are aware that their wages from work is the only safety net in their old age while married women can rely on their children for support.

Emotion work: costs and benefits

Some women have been fortunate enough to be able to appropriate strategies to integrate the two worlds of workplace and home by resorting to institutional care, either state-sponsored or privately-run childcare centres. In the industrialized countries of the Western hemisphere, the increasing availability of institutionalized childcare arrangements and part-time work has made it possible for women to take on paid work (Bernhardt 1993; England 1996). The experience of Asian women has been different as they have the option of relying on informal childcare arrangements such as neighbours, grandparents and other relatives (Huang and Yeoh 1997; Yeoh and Huang 1995).

Others have been able to purchase care work through the services rendered by women migrants, a topic that will be discussed at length in Chapters 4 and 6 in this volume. For the middle-class Southeast Asian working woman, harnessing the labour of other women is one strategy to better manage the two roles of worker and caregiver. For them, a live-in domestic worker is indispensable. The domestic worker relieves her female employer of a myriad of household chores, including the care she would have had to give to her children, if she had not been working (Huang *et al.* 2007).

Bélanger and Oudin (2007) narrate how Vietnamese women have tasted success as a result of being able to capitalize on the multitude of political and economic changes because of the economic reform (*doi moi*). But many of these women have only been able to maintain their jobs because they have been able to take advantage of the burgeoning supply of domestic helpers, caregivers and tutors who have contributed significantly to their capacity to balance the worker and mother roles.

But beyond exploiting the labour of these poorer women without whom middle-class women would not be able to pursue their own careers, employing a foreign domestic worker is a marker of middle-class identity, as the working woman is at liberty to transfer the execution of emotional labour to another (Chin 1998). Since these employed women engage in emotion work such as the care provided to children, employers may use various strategies to ascertain loyalty and gratitude on the part of their helpers. In Indonesia, for example, gift-giving is integral to forging fictive kinship ties in the employer–servant relationship. While the relationship is marked by paternalism, as suggested by Weix (2000), or of a patron–client nature, for a working woman, this practice is a constant reminder of her dependence on an outsider.

Middle-class women, however, are not the only women balancing the caregiver and worker roles. The very women whose domestic labour they purchase face their own unique set of struggles in caring for their own children, a topic described in Chapter 3 in this volume. But by and large, the employer stands to gain in this relationship; although she may have a domestic worker to help her manage her own home, the woman whom she employs is faced with the harder task of having to nurture her own children at a distance. As compared to the workplace setting where male-dominated structures manipulate women's emotions, social and cultural expectations thrust upon working women in the context of the home have forced them to become manipulators of other women's emotions at the expense of exploiting their labour.

But not all women see the employment of the services of non-relatives as a remedy to the problems they face. Some women are not keen on handing over the role of caregiver to a non-relative such as a domestic worker. Devasahayam (2003b), in her interviews with working Malay women in urban Malaysia, voiced their fear if their own children developed affectionate ties with the domestic worker. Caught in this bind, working mothers would go to great lengths to affirm their kin ties with their own husbands and children by cooking the main dishes for a meal and making sure that they spend time with their families after work each day and over the weekends. Cooking, in particular, holds cultural import for Malay women as they spoke of the food they produced as extension of themselves and, when shared with family members, intensified the forging of kinship between these women and their kin, as discussed earlier in this chapter. Since cooking is an activity invested with emotion and the sharing and presentation of food mobilize strong emotions, this impels women to execute this task themselves rather than leaving it to non-relatives.

Beyond bonding through their role as food providers, a woman's emotions are called forth in their maternal role as producers of the 'perfect child' (Hirao 2007: 69). This puts added pressure on women as caregivers, as in the case of Japan with the burgeoning growth of private schools which emphasize performance. Handbooks churned out by the Ministry of Education, Culture, Sports, Science and Technology (MEXT) detail the '"proper" guidance for parenting and disciplining at home' (ibid.: 71). In this case, women become the main educational agents for their own children and the educational excellence achieved by their children is linked to their own success and emotional satisfaction as caregivers. Women in Japan may in some cases have to reassess their career goals, however, this is within a culture which is slower to change than most Asian countries, where women are balancing parenting and career demands through the use of maids, which is not common in Japan.

In cases of divorce in some countries such as Singapore, career women are disadvantaged as illustrated by Ong (2007). Decisions made in the Singapore courts have used this as a measure to determine if a woman should undertake custody for her child(ren) in the case of a divorce. Here, the idea that the biological mother is the most suitable parent to undertake the primary caregiver role does not automatically impinge on the court's decision in terms of claims to custody. Rather, a woman has to be able to demonstrate an emotional bond with her child(ren) through care and concern at the day-to-day level in order to influence the court's decision. In other words, if a woman is able to show that she has performed the maternal role without letting her career interfere with her familial commitments, this is most likely to have a positive impact on the court's decision in her favour.

Governments also see importance in emotional bonding between parents, especially mothers, and children. Stivens (2007: 36, citing from 'Strike balance between work and family, officers told', *New Straits Times*, 19 October 2000) gives the example of Malaysia where government department heads have been urged to encourage their staff to 'spend more time with their families . . . "because a person's emotional stability would come from a stable family"'.

Conclusion

The situation in Asia is rapidly changing as regards the work–life balance. Various governments in the region are recognizing the fact that women are significantly a valuable asset in the workforce. Yet women are increasingly less responsive towards family policies owing to potential career development and consequent lifestyle demands. This is particularly the case in global cities dominating Asia. Younger women across Asia are demanding a different pattern in terms of both domestic and career expectations. As with many countries, the operation of policy frequently lags behind life patterns, and governments in the region such as in Singapore and Vietnam realize that the expectations of women need to be met. This is particularly recognized in Annual National Day Speeches in Singapore. Religions such as Islam in Malaysia and Indonesia and political ideology as in Japan continue to act against women's interests. The longer term is likely to see an assessment of the work–life balance similar to the experiences of working women in the West.

3 Globalization, the feminization of migration and emotional labour

Theresa Devasahayam

Introduction

Globalization has made migrating for work a reality. While opening up national borders as a result of free trade agreements across countries, enabling the free flow of goods and services, creating global outsourcing, and triggering the growth of international corporations and organizations, globalization has simultaneously created work opportunities for many seeking employment abroad (Felker 2003; Marsh *et al*. 1999; Tsai and Tsay 2004). It has been argued by some scholars that globalization has had an uneven impact on the countries of the developing world. East and Southeast Asia, however, have been presented as counter-evidence, showing that these regions have largely benefited from economic global trends (Apodaca 2002). Primarily, it has been shown that with globalization came fluidity in the international economy, resulting in a wide range of jobs (Gereffi and Sturgeon 2004).

In Asia, women from skilled and low-skilled backgrounds have found work in a multitude of sectors as a result of globalization. In fact, the region has become a nucleus of migratory labour flows in recent decades (Huguet 2003; Piper 2004a; Wong *et al*. 2003). It is not uncommon for poor women to leave their countries to secure employment in the more affluent economies because of the demand for domestic work. In the richer countries, the lack of state provision of childcare facilities has forced many women to turn to foreign domestic workers (Wong 1992, cited in Chan 2005). Gripped by the rising cost of living, the need to contribute to the household income, and the fervour to become careerists, women from the more affluent economies have turned to the employment of temporary women migrants to whom they have transferred their own domestic demands.

In Singapore, for example, this trend toward balancing work and family is reinforced by social pressures to 'build . . . a nest egg for themselves and their children' (Mathiaparanam 2008: 45). Thus, women migrants from the poorer economies in the region play a critical role in enabling women from the developed economies to engage in paid work outside the home (Chan and Wong 2005). Furthermore, in employing women migrants as caretakers of their own children, middle-class women in the destination countries are appropriating the nurturing qualities of women migrating from low-income countries, thereby reproducing social and cultural norms placed on them.

Among women migrants, thus, '"selling" their care work as both unpaid (house)wife and paid care worker' in the destination countries 'enables them to provide care work to their famil[ies]' back home (Lauser 2008: 103). In this sense, economic migration is conflated with emotional migration among women migrants, as reiterated by Lauser (2008, as cited in Huang *et al.* 2008) and Yea (2008, as cited in Huang *et al.* 2008). But such women who migrate carry the additional burden of children left behind. This chapter shows that in spite of becoming transnational workers, the demands of carrying out the nurturer and caregiver role persist for these women. While the constraints they face are not very different from women who stay behind with their families, there is the added dimension of tension in having to carry out their nurturer role in spite of being physically separated from their families. As Ahmed, Castañeda, Fortier and Sheller (2004: 2) suggest:

> [We should then view] home [and in this case, family] and migration in terms of a plurality of experiences, histories and constituencies . . . The task is therefore not to categorize 'home' [and, in this case, their families left behind] as a condition distinct from 'migration', or to order them in terms of their relative value or cultural salience, but to ask how uprootings and regroundings are enacted – affectively, materially and symbolically – in relation to one another.

But engaging in the care sector poses conflicts for migrant women. Women find themselves providing for the needs of other women's children while constrained in providing care and concern to their own children because of the distance (Hochschild 2003b). Furthermore, in spite of engaging in care work, their identities as workers are emphasized above their identities as mothers. To put it another way, transnational workers engaging in low-end domestic work operate within a context of emotions and yet their capacity to express themselves fully in this context is constrained by their worker identity. For many of them, they provide care on behalf of other women without being assured of the emotions that they would have received from their own children. Thus, migration decentres the family as a site of stability, comfort and love for these women. By no means does the structure of the family change as a result of undergoing considerable tension and shifts, as this chapter shows. Conversely, in spite of the ruptures on the family as a result of migration, women continue to be the focal point in family relationships.

The bulk of low-skilled women who migrate for wage work are mothers but who are not privileged to take their children along with them to the countries they find work. While poor women feel the tensions of having to carry out their nurturer role at a distance, skilled women who migrate for work generally move with their children so the pressures of absence and guilt do not apply in the same way. But in contrast to the experiences of low-skilled migrant women, this group of women have to confront a workplace dominated by men. As such, women who migrate for work, whether skilled or low-skilled, have a heavy price to pay in their own families, as this chapter demonstrates. But whether low-skilled or skilled, women migrants have been found to exercise agency and, in turn, make meaning of their experiences independently from the 'dominant social order' (de Certeau 1984: xiii).

The feminization of migration

Although cross-border migration is not a new phenomenon in Asia, contemporary migration trends in response to globalization have seen increasing number of women migrants as compared in the past when the pool of migrants consisted mainly of men (Castles and Miller 2003; Huguet 2003; Jolly and Reeves 2005; Piper 2004a). Generally, migrant women are employed chiefly in low-end or 3D (dangerous, difficult and dirty) jobs or traditionally 'female' occupations characterized by low wages, poor work conditions, and lacking employment benefits (United Nations 2005). In particular, women migrants dominate the domestic work sector (Tan 2001, as cited in Huguet 2003), although there is a smaller proportion employed in the entertainment industry (see Hilsdon 2007). Moreover, often these women are employed on temporary work arrangements and are expected to return to their countries on completion of their employment contracts.

While the majority of these women have low levels of education, women migrating from the Philippines are an exception. Among them, many are tertiary-educated but they end up as domestic workers overseas because they are remunerated much more in the domestic work sector abroad compared to finding jobs at home with their level of skills. Hence, migrant women do not undertake low-skilled jobs because they are naturally suited to them but because women enter these sectors already determined as inferior workers in the labour market (Resurreccion 2009). For this reason, Oishi (2005: 187) notes: 'Migration leads to downward social mobility, since migrant women tend to be concentrated in sectors that are not commensurate with their professional qualifications.'

Source countries in the Asian region for unskilled women migrants employed particularly in domestic work and on other short-term contracts include Bangladesh, Cambodia, Indonesia, Malaysia, Myanmar, Nepal, Pakistan, the Philippines, and Thailand. Popular destination countries for these women migrants include India, Hong Kong, Japan, Malaysia, Singapore, Taiwan, Thailand, as well as the countries in the Middle East (Asia Development Outlook 2008b). In Singapore alone, one in six households employs a foreign domestic worker. Currently, more than 190,000 foreign domestic workers are employed in the country (Devasahayam 2010).

While there has been an increase in the numbers of women going abroad to seek employment, the percentage of women migrants in Asia is much smaller than that in the rest of the world (Global Migration Group 2008). In Asia alone, however, the Economic and Social Commission for the Asia Pacific database for 2000–2005 records about 600,000 women from Indonesia, the Philippines, and Sri Lanka migrating abroad in search of paid work in 2000 while the numbers rose to 668,000 in 2005 (see Table 3.1). From these countries, women form the majority of the migrants: Indonesia (79 per cent), the Philippines (72 per cent), and Sri Lanka (62 per cent). From the Philippines alone, about 4.2 to 6.4 million

Table 3.1 Number and percentage of women in labour flows in Asia, 2000–2007

		2000	2001	2002	2003	2004	2005	2006	2007
Indonesia	Number	297255	..	367501	..	334700	324902	..	..
	Percentage	68.3	..	76.5	..	87.5	68.5	..	..
Philippines	Number	178323	186018	208278	175103	209458	205206	184454	146337
	Percentage	23.8	72.0	72.8	72.5	74.3	72.2	59.5	47.8
Sri Lanka	Number	122395	124200	133251	135338	134010	137394	113236	..
	Percentage	40.2	40.3	39.5	39.2	38.4	37.3	35.7	..

Source: Database on Asian migration maintained at ESCAP; Indonesia, IOM, ESCAP *et al.* (2008): Situation Report on International Migration in East and South-east Asia, Bangkok, taken from United Nations Economic and Social Commission for Asia and the Pacific (UNESCAP) 'Key Trends and Challenges on International Migration and Development in Asia and the Pacific', paper presented at Expert Group Meeting on International Migration and Development in Asia and the Pacific, Population Division, Department of Economic and Social Affairs, Bangkok, September 2008.

women are working overseas as foreign domestic workers, constituting a sizeable proportion of the estimated 7–8 million Filipinos working abroad (Wee and Sim 2004). In fact, the numbers of Filipinos leaving the country have not declined as estimates from 2008 show that almost 1.4 million found jobs abroad while in 2007 the numbers were 1.1 million ('Southeast Asia – Migration News/Migration Dialogue' 2009).

Globalization has also meant that skilled female workers travel for work. But by possessing skills required in many labour sectors, these women are usually subject to a different set of labour rules in the receiving countries. Moreover, many of them are granted the option of taking up permanent residence or citizenship in the labour-receiving countries. Many professional women migrants travel for work but mostly for shorter periods. But if they did travel for lengthy periods, many have the option of taking their families with them unlike unskilled women migrants. In most instances, however, the norm is for men to travel and take their families with them while women play the supportive role to a working husband (Willis and Yeoh 2000; Wong *et al.* 2003; Yeoh and Khoo 1998) although this pattern is changing. It is these men who leave the management of the household to their wives.

While migration trends in the region show an increase in the number of women migrants, it must be emphasized that '[the] migration [process] is not a "gender-neutral" phenomenon' (Global Migration Group 2008: 45). The next two sections of this chapter demonstrate how the reasons for migrating and the experiences encountered by migrants in their jobs differ considerably for women and men.

The impulse to migrate

For poor women, migrating for work is seen to lift their families out of poverty. Each year, millions of dollars worth of remittances are sent back to their families and communities. According to World Bank estimates, migrant Filipino workers working in over 200 countries abroad remitted a record US$ 18.268 billion in 2008 (Devasahayam 2009b). The amount of remittances sent back to the Philippines, however, varies depending on the migrants' skills and the destination economies where the migrants take up employment (Tan 2001, as cited in Go 2002).

It is for this reason it has been argued that migration is linked to family survival more than state-level rationality (Castles 1998, as cited in Wong *et al.* 2003). These remittances have gone into feeding and educating children, ensuring health-care for their families and relatives, and improving the standard of living of their families owing to the higher rate of use of consumer durables (United Nations Economic and Social Commission for Asia and the Pacific 2008). In Sri Lanka, research has found that migration for work has enabled families to purchase land, construct a new or better house, buy electricity for the household, and build a modern latrine system (Gamburd 2000). Furthermore, it has been argued that the adoption of a new lifestyle marked by the higher consumption of material goods, has strengthened the family through the prudent use of remittances.

Interestingly, gender is an important dimension in the social behaviour of sending remittances back to families. It has been found that women remit less to their families than migrant men owing to the fact that they earn less than their male counterparts. But in proportion to what they earn, data shows that women remit much more than what men would remit to their families (Global Commission on International Migration 2005; Osaki 1999). In addition, women migrants have been shown to remit more regularly and consistently than male migrants since migrant women tend to retain stronger links with their families (Hugo 2002). This should come as no surprise since women retain stronger ties with their relatives at home than male migrants.

Women's behaviour in relation to remittances has been found to be linked to altruism. In Thailand, for example, providing material support through remittances is a way for women to acquire religious merit for their families (Vanwey 2004). Others may remit so that their families allow them to migrate for work (Curran 1995, as cited in Vanwey 2004). Others, however, have argued that altruism does not explain remittance behaviour; instead, as in many other receiving countries in the world, the remittance becomes necessary to ensure that the surrogate caregivers in the sending countries continue to provide care for the left-behind children in the absence of the migrant parent (Secondi 1997).

Many poor women are forced to find work abroad because of the lack of suitable jobs in their home countries. There is also the assumption that migrating for work is a quick way of making vast sums of money (Gamburd 2000). Job segregation and discrimination in respect to training as a result of gender stereotyping are other factors that push women to seek work abroad (Sobritchea 2007). Related to this, women have been found to have limited choices in access to jobs as compared to their male counterparts. In addition, many are not able to engage in small-scale business ventures in their home countries because they do not possess sufficient collateral to secure loans, to which men have greater access because of discriminatory customary and legal laws. Moreover, it was found that women instead of their husbands tend to leave for wage work abroad because the cost involved for them to go overseas is not as large as when men migrate for employment (Gamburd 2000).

While the economic impulse to migrate forms the primary factor for seeking out employment abroad, there are also personal reasons. Research in Sri Lanka shows that marital problems such as wife beating, alcoholism, infidelity and desertion aside from economic hardship are among other multiple reasons pushing women to find work overseas (ibid.). In this sense, migrant women must be seen to have great potential for agency in that they are 'capable of acting in their own interest' (Piper and Roces 2003: 9). As such, women also found work abroad to fulfil their own desires and escape brutality and oppression. Thus, women migrants are frequently expressing 'agency' as migrants. Therefore, it is a misconception to see women migrants as victims.

Many have returned home with skills, experiences and ideas which they picked up as migrants. As a consequence, they have greater decision-making power in their families and are better equipped to advise their family members and communities on various matters. Furthermore, while actively contributing to raising the levels of well-being of the family, the status of many of these women has been enhanced in the family and community (United Nations Economic and Social Commission for Asia and the Pacific 2008). Oishi (2005) remarks how many of her informants from the Philippines and Sri Lanka spoke about developing self-confidence and independence. Filipino female entertainers in Japan sought to work abroad not only for their families but also to carve out an identity for themselves (Tyner 2002). Clearly work opportunities abroad have enabled these women to exercise their agency to change the course of their lives.

Because of the demand for labour in certain sectors in countries abroad, some governments have seized the opportunity to encourage migration especially if the country has a less than thriving economy and is unable to absorb workers. For example, the Philippines has been actively encouraging migration for employment since 1974 (*Migration News* 1996). As a result, the Philippine Overseas Employment Administration (POEA), a government agency, was set up to oversee the overseas employment of Filipinos. In this respect, Sri Lanka has also launched a national labour migration policy with the expressed aim of adhering to principles, policies and guidelines articulated in international labour migration instruments. Others have lifted bans on exporting labour abroad. Such is the case of Nepal. In 2007, the Foreign Employment Act was established to reverse the gender discrimination previously linked to the foreign employment sector as it lifted all restrictions on women leaving the country to take up employment abroad (UNIFEM n.d.). Moreover, government recognition of the role of migrant workers in the country's economic development has led to initiatives such as the provision of pre-departure training to potential migrant workers.

Notable examples of sending countries with formal pre-departure training programmes organized by the government are Indonesia, the Philippines and Sri Lanka (Gender and Development InBrief 2005). That governments stand to gain from the remittances sent home by migrant workers invariably is the reason why there have been efforts to govern migration flows. Economic growth in the state of Kerala in India, for example, has been linked to the remittances sent back by migrant workers in the Gulf, although there has been a plea made for the government to be more proactive in converting savings into productive investments (Kannan and Hari 2002). In the case of the Philippines, remittances form a significant portion of the revenue of the government and have doubled from US$ 6.2 billion in 2000 to US$ 15.3 billion in 2006 (Asian Development Outlook 2008b). In a similar vein, the government of Sri Lanka acknowledges the critical role its migrant workers play in the country's economic development which led to the establishment of its national labour migration policy (International Labour Organization 2009b).

Migration and (un)changing gender relations

For migrant women, whether they are professional or low-skilled, mobility in search of employment impacts on family structure because mothers tend to be the focal point of social relationships in the family. Because of the critical role they play in the family, if they are separated from the family for extended periods, the family has to adapt accordingly. The solution among them is to leave their children in the care of other women, mostly female relatives (United Nations Economic and Social Commission for Asia and the Pacific 2008). For these women, thus, migrating for work comes with heavy social costs, especially for married women migrants who face tremendous challenges in playing the maternal role to their families. Beyond playing the maternal role, these women struggle with engaging in emotional labour, a vital way of building intimacy and closeness with others especially family members because of being separated through distance. In contrast, the impact on the family by unmarried migrants is less pronounced (Asis *et al.* 2004). The same trend applies to male migrants whether they are married or unmarried.

Thus migration for employment has not altered dominant gender ideologies pertaining to women's and men's roles in the family. While the driving force behind migrating for work among women migrants is to enable their children to have a better life, ironically many are forced to be separated from their own families. This is the case for low-skilled women migrants, in particular, because they are not allowed to take their children to the countries of employment according to the labour rules of the receiving countries. But women also migrate in their role as daughters aside from being mothers. Thai daughters, more than sons, see their productive capacity as a means to lift their natal families out of poverty (Clawen 2002). In the same vein, they continue to provide emotional support to their families back home.

On the part of women migrants, it is not uncommon to find them denying the emotional costs of separation. While they acknowledged the pain felt by children, they consciously juxtaposed this emotional loss against the material gain in transnational family life. Such were the responses of the Filipina women migrants working in Los Angeles and Rome (Salazar Parreñas 2001a). Similar rationalizations were articulated by Sri Lankan women migrants in an effort to ward off the criticisms they received (Gamburd 2000).

Tensions arise because playing the maternal role carries with it specific meaning in many cultures. By Filipino standards, Lauser (2008: 91) describes: 'a good wife is someone who protects the interests of her husband and who manages the household and children efficiently'. There are no constraints on women wishing to engage in wage work as long as they continue to play the caregiver and nurturer role to their family members and manage the household. These expectations of a Filipino woman continue to hold even if she is a migrant worker. Among such women, 'good' mothering entails engaging in activities of '"multiple burden and sacrifice", spending "quality time" during brief home visits, and reaffirming the "mother influence and presence" through surrogate figures and regular communication with their children' (Sobritchea 2007: 179) – activities which demand feelings of warmth and yet frustration on the part of the women.

The sacrifices these women make include not spending the little they make as foreign domestic workers on personal effects such as toiletries and the like, but instead sending their earnings home to their loved ones. Suffering verbal abuse from their employers was mentioned as another sacrifice these women make.

Often they resurrect the concept of 'long suffering' so as to keep focused on their intentions for working abroad (ibid.: 182). In spite of engaging in these activities, many report feeling a sense of failure in their maternal role, especially if they have handed over the basic responsibility of providing care to their relatives. In fact, leaving their children with relatives is culturally acceptable since childrearing is often seen as a collective practice conducted within the wider social framework of extended families and neighbours (Devasahayam 2004; Lauser 2008). Nonetheless, migrant women expressed guilt especially since they did not care for their own children while instead providing care to the children of other women (Ehrenreich and Hochschild 2003).

In spite of being separated from their families in time and space, many women migrants have been able to overcome the conflicts inherent in the unique situation they have found themselves by devising various means of being good mothers at a distance. For this reason, many of these women are not victims of circumstances in which they find themselves; instead they have been innovative in their response in coping with their multifaceted roles.

In a study conducted on Indonesian domestic worker mothers in Singapore, Rahman and Devasahayam (2004) found that sustaining regular communication was integral to carrying out the maternal role. The women interviewed all said that telephone calls, letters and sending out sms-es were critical to strengthening familial ties and mother–child bonding because it not only enables expressions of love to be demonstrated but allows them to advise and keep up-to-date with their children's development and progress. Concomitantly irregular communication is seen to compromise the mother–child relationship and there is a constant fear of losing the kinship relationship. In a sense, motherhood for these women means: 'I'm here, but I'm there', as explained by Hondagneu-Sotelo and Avila (1997: 558) and, as such, they 'advocate more elastic definitions of motherhood, including forms that may include long spatial and temporal separations of mother and children'. Furthermore, for them, there is an implicit understanding that the family is created processually and is never a fixed entity.

Distance, however, is not a barrier. As suggested by Ahmed, Castañeda, Fortier and Sheller (2004), any effort to close the physical space between the woman and her family back home is an attempt to 'blur the distinction between [the] here and there'. For this reason, how the various communication means are deployed serves to dislodge an often emphasized notion in the literature on transnationalism that location is a 'discrete entity' (ibid.: 4). Thus, transnational mothers invest considerable effort in the mothering role, using every means of communication available to them to enact the *experience of being* with their loved ones.

This is critical especially since for these women, the reason why they work goes far beyond furnishing their families with material gains. Staying in touch with their families back home entails their emotional labour as much as effort and discipline. If their children did not reciprocate emotionally, often these women were left feeling angry and frustrated. It is for this reason that many women confessed guilt and regret in not being able to fulfil the caring and nurturing roles as they wanted because of not being physically present with their families.

Migrating for work also causes tensions in the relationship between husband and wife in the family context. By engaging in productive labour, women migrants have called into question the male as breadwinner role model. In interviews conducted of approximately 60 families of women migrants in a village in Sri Lanka, Gamburd (2000) found that when a woman migrated for work, this was an admission on the part of the family that her husband could not provide for the family, thereby challenging his capacity to be the breadwinner. In the community, migrant women 'lost a measure of honor, a blemish offset but not erased by financial success' (ibid.: 186), often inviting gossip as well because a migrant woman was perceived to be contesting the gendered division of labour characterized by women as the primary nurturers and caregivers. In this case, a man usually does not assume a woman's primary role although there have been exceptions. But these exceptions tended to be overlooked by the families left behind, possibly to preserve the masculine image of men (ibid.).

Nevertheless, if a man migrates for work, it is interesting to note that usually the wives end up assuming the roles their husbands previously held in the absence of the father figure. Thus among married migrant women, husbands seldom embrace the reproductive roles of their wives. As such, the mother's migration has a greater impact on family structure than the father's migration (Battistella and Conaco 1998). In contrast, married male migrants with children do not feel a similar social pressure; if they are away from their families for work, their children only perceive this to be an extension of their breadwinner role (Salazar Parreñas 2005).

Although women migrants have not abandoned their reproductive role toward their families by attempting to keep up the maternal role at a distance, children have been found to reinforce the dominant gender model of women as caregivers and men as breadwinners. The book *Children of Global Migration* (2005) by Rhacel Salazar Parreñas analyses the different expectations of children of global Filipina women migrants of their mothers and fathers taking up work abroad. The children Salazar Parreñas interviewed were agreeable to their fathers pursuing careers, while they saw their mothers as being forced to find work abroad because of poverty in spite of their mothers having become the breadwinners of the family. Another point of interest is that while they saw fathers as exercising their right to work by entering the labour force, they saw their mothers as risking their roles as caregivers by taking on work abroad, thus showing that children continued to see their mothers as primarily caregivers and nurturers.

Thus, a woman who works abroad is perceived by her children 'as oppositional to the interest of the family and acceptable only if done in desperation. This difference exists because fathers subscribe to gender boundaries and mothers break them when they migrate' (ibid.: 66). While cultural norms continue to reinforce gender by placing different expectations on the sexes, children of migrant parents also often applied double standards to their parents, thereby perpetuating gender roles and forcing women to see the work they engage in as their secondary role and identity. Furthermore, the income a working woman generates does not displace the income of the father, in spite of the fact that the income of the woman migrant is integral to the survival of the family.

There are other contexts in which low-skilled women migrants have not abandoned their reproductive role in spite of engaging in productive work abroad. While marital strains back home are the main reason for these women to seek out emotional relationships with other men in the destination country, conflicts arise particularly if these women have left their own children behind. Research on Filipina entertainers working in South Korea found that these women are faced with two dilemmas: maintaining their relationships with their own children left behind from a previous marriage and their ability to continue their breadwinner role by sending back remittances to help their own natal families (Yea 2008). While in some cases, these women were able to rely on their new husbands to provide for their old families back home, there were others who were not as fortunate. Yea provides ethnographic examples of Filipina entertainers who found their new husbands stopping them from sending remittances home.

No matter how these women strategized to sustain their families back home, their new relationships created a break with their old kin ties back home, thereby preventing them from playing the maternal role as culturally expected. Interestingly in this case, women themselves perpetuate gender norms although they have the liberty to turn their backs on their own families back home and yet this is not their chosen path. Notions of personal and collective constructions on who they are and the roles they are expected to fulfil in spite of being in a foreign place do not change. Instead they realize their sense of self both in the relationships left behind as well as in the new relationships they form.

Conflicts also arise among women who migrate with their children. Ironically women working in the entertainment industry also face the dilemma of being expected to shed their identity as mothers completely in spite of being physically with their children. Among Filipina mothers employed in the highly sexualized entertainment industry in the state of Sabah of East Malaysia, 'the prescriptions of the entertainment industry for the "young, single, childless [not to mention sexy and alluring] performer"' have made it difficult for the married migrant women to carry out 'traditional' forms of mothering because definitions of motherhood are in constant conflict with that of the professional entertainer (Hilsdon 2007: 19). These women are constantly forced to keep up the appearance of being sexually alluring so as to satisfy a predominantly male clientele (ibid.). If they are found incapable of keeping their own natal families' concerns separate from the demands placed on them by their employers, their efficiency as workers is called to question. Thus, working in the entertainment industry presents a particular set of obstacles to women migrants as motherhood in its more traditional forms, as defined, perceived and understood by them, is frequently contested and reconstituted.

Balancing work and family: the experiences of skilled women workers

Invariably, gender continues to be a strong variable ordering the family lives of professional working women as well. If they have to travel to find work, these women make a conscious effort to arrange their travel schedules around their children and often call home to check on the children while away on business trips (Huang *et al.* 2007). The distance between them and their children does not deter them from carrying out the emotional work of caring. Some working women have also been found to balance work obligations against domestic labour demands by keeping strictly to their busy schedules and returning home swiftly because of their children (Lai and Huang 2004).

While some professional women have integrated the two worlds of workplace and home by resorting to institutional care, either state-sponsored or privately run childcare centres, this option is not suitable if the professional woman has to travel for work. Instead the choice would be to rely on informal childcare arrangements such as neighbours, grandparents and other relatives or employ a live-in foreign domestic worker to take on the caregiver role in their absence (Huang and Yeoh 1998; Yeoh and Huang 1995).

It is for these women – the 'new middle-class jugglers' – that the help of a foreign domestic worker becomes essential to enable the professional woman to engage in wage work (Litt and Zimmerman 2003; Yeoh *et al.* 1999). On the indispensability of paid labour provided by foreign women from the poorer economies, Singaporean women see 'a live-in transnational domestic worker [as] a vital strategy to manage the demands' of work and family (Huang *et al.* 2007: 266). The domestic worker relieves her female employer of a myriad of household chores, including the care she would give to her children, if she had not been working (ibid.). Some women also reported that transferring the household chores to a foreign domestic worker has freed up time for them to be with their children (Yeoh *et al.*1999).

But while employing foreign women to carry out the caregiver role has benefited scores of professional women in affluent countries, this has done little to alter dominant gender ideologies on women's and men's roles in the family. In fact, it has been argued that it is the option of purchasing the reproductive labour of other women that has caused a 'lag in the emergence of egalitarian gender relations in the family' (Asis 2003: 109).

Furthermore, the presence of an outsider in the home may be seen to be invasive of the private space of couple and their family because the 'private sphere of the employer [has become] the public sphere of the employee' (Gill 1994: 9). In this case, the intimate spaces of the home linked to the expression of emotions between members of the family are interrupted by the presence of an outsider.

As much as employers are forced to adjust to the presence of a non-relative in the home, there is also adjustment and, perhaps, uncertainty on the part of the domestic worker as to how she should relate to her employer(s) because working in a home blurs the boundaries between home and workplace. But according to the experiences of some foreign domestic workers, their employer's families have become 'like family' to the domestic worker because of the 'trust, openness and concern' their employers have demonstrated toward these women migrants (Asis *et al.* 2004: 210).

To put it another way, 'homing desires' develop: 'desires to feel at home achieved by physically or symbolically (re)constituting spaces which provide some kind of ontological security in the context of migration' (Fortier 2004: 115). If this is the case, the workplace becomes home for them – a context in which they do not feel inhibited expressing their feelings and emotions and bonding with members of the family whom they work for, even though they are aware that the relationships they build may be dissolved at any time (Chan 2005).

There are numerous narratives of domestic workers who have formed family-like relationships with their employers' children as well as other members of the family. Crisanta Sampang, a former foreign domestic worker employed in Singapore in the 1980s, relates her feelings and affections for the people for whom she worked in her book *Maid in Singapore*. This is what she says of her 'grandma' (Sampang 2005: 51–2):

> Grandma was a skilled housekeeper, a loving Mum, a doting grandmother, a patient teacher. It wasn't what I had expected at all. Other maids from my agency had warned me about grandmothers – those malevolent, elderly women who were the curse of foreign domestics . . .
>
> My Grandma turned out to be different, and I immediately fell in love with her. Grandma didn't command or instruct, but quietly set an example of cleanliness, speed and efficiency for me to follow. It was an unspoken challenge she offered, and which I accepted . . . Grandma was always cheerful, and generous. She would often give me things she knew I'd appreciate and watch with pleasure the joy with which I received them.
>
> Grandma used the different special occasions throughout the year as an excuse to buy me clothes. I always get red packets from Grandma during Chinese New Year. I left Singapore for Vancouver a few months after Grandma passed away, but I still cry each time I think about her. I still miss her, even today.

Because domestic work and care work entail feelings of warmth and affection, not all women welcome with open arms the labour of other women. Some women have viewed domestic workers as a threat to their maternal role should their own children develop affectionate ties with the domestic worker (Chan 2005; Devasahayam 2003). If they are forced to rely on non-relatives such as temporary women migrants to help provide care for their own children, there is usually a great deal of hesitation or even reluctance among these women. For these women, the presence of an outsider in the household calls into question what it means to be 'family' and the extent to which they are able to independently provide emotional labour to their own children without having to depend on non-kin (Asis *et al.* 2004).

But employing women migrants to carry out care work in the family comes with other concerns. There have been questions about the kinds of values foreign women may potentially transfer to their employers' children. There have been debates especially on the social impact women migrants have on the social fabric of Singapore families (Yeoh *et al.* 1999) since the majority of domestic workers come from countries that do not share cultural commonalities with the countries where they take up employment. For this reason, some women have consciously decided not to purchase care work provided by non-relatives.

Conclusion

As a result of globalization, the world of many contemporary Asian women, both migrant and non-migrant, has become marked by the shifting boundaries of the concepts of public and private and the ongoing reconfigurations of 'home', 'domesticity', 'worker', 'father', 'mother' and 'child' (Stivens 2007: 29). Among women migrants, because migration entails separation, this has reordered their lives and, in turn, the lives of their families in different ways. Working across transnational borders has led to 'a dynamic process of reconfiguration' of traditional forms of raising families (Sobritchea 2007: 179). But the reconfiguration of gender roles depends largely on which parent migrates for work. In the case of women migrating, they almost always end up negotiating long-distance mothering.

For many Asian women, globalization has enabled women to take on wage work and thereby helped them sustain their families. But wage work now has the potential of fracturing the family (Yeoh 2005). Women find that their emotions among family members are torn. But most women, migrants or otherwise, have been able to reconcile the conflicting experiences they face. For the unskilled migrant women workers, the objective of material security for their families is the central factor in their acceptance of the conditions in which they find themselves. It is for this reason that a paradox arises when 'the achievement of financial security for the sake of the children goes hand-in-hand with an increase in emotional insecurity . . . [and] . . . the loss of intimacy in many families' (Salazar Parreñas 2001a: 149). Their educated sisters also have to pay a price in their quest for professional recognition and financial independence. Because cultural and social constructs demand that they continue to play the caregiver role in spite of taking on wage work, this means that they too have to engage in the balancing act of mother and worker.

4 Human rights and female migrant labour in Asia

Theresa Devasahayam

Introduction

It is widely acknowledged that supra-state institutions are critical in the struggle to protect migrant worker rights, however, the role of international legal frameworks has generally been weak in this region. Promoting human rights has been the long-standing goal of the United Nations starting with the 1948 Universal Declaration of Human Rights. The basic principle underlying the concept of human rights emphasizes the notion of universality; in other words, the concept of human rights is linked to a 'common humanity' rather than a common citizenship (Grant 2005a: 16). The notions of equality, non-discrimination and inclusion are also central to the concept of human rights ('Know Your Rights', G.A. res. 217A (III), U.N. Doc A/810 at 71 1948).

Despite the existence of such universal declarations of human rights, human rights violations are rampant among low-skilled migrant workers across Asia. Migrant rights abuses are reported periodically in the media in both receiving and sending countries. These reported cases, however, are those that are known, resulting in the perpetrators being charged according to the laws of the receiving countries. But, in reality, the majority of cases of rights abuse do not surface because of the nature of the work and the asymmetrical power relationships between employer and worker, making it difficult, if not impossible, for the worker to report the abuse.

Attempts to address migrant worker rights violations have occurred at various levels. Some labour-sending countries have been proactive in reducing the abuses encountered by their migrants. The Philippines has installed numerous labour control measures administered through the state-controlled department, the Philippine Overseas Employment Administration. The country has been assertive in ensuring protection for its citizen migrants through organizing high-level missions to address migrant welfare, enforcing model contracts for migrant protection, and regulating private recruitment agencies. Others such as Indonesia have resorted to establishing pre-departure programmes to empower migrant workers by providing information and increasing awareness of key issues related to labour practices. But there are limits to managing labour from the sending country since many abuses erupt in the receiving country. In some cases, labour-sending countries have insisted on labour-receiving governments addressing migrant worker abuses promptly lest the situation lead to 'irritation' in bilateral ties (*The Malaysian Insider*, 29 January 2010).

Generally, however, the governments of many receiving destinations in the Asian region have been slow to react to the need to protect foreign nationals, arguing that migrant workers are protected by national laws and labour policies, although in reality they are not because of their immigrant status (Piper 2004a, 2004b; Yeoh *et al.* 2004). Furthermore, many of these governments have argued that labour practices are private sector business practices, and that governments should not intervene in order to ensure a market-oriented system. For example, in Bangladesh, India, Pakistan and Sri Lanka, 90 per cent of migrant labour is recruited by private labour agencies (United Nations Economic and Social Commission for Asia and the Pacific 2008).

Bilateral agreements have also been deployed to protect migrant labour rights governing recruitment, employment contracts, conditions of work, return migration provisions and jurisdiction matters related to transnational labour practices by some countries. But they tend to be the exception rather than the rule in the Asian region. The few countries that have signed bilateral agreements are Malaysia with Bangladesh, Cambodia, Sri Lanka and Vietnam; Thailand with Cambodia, Laos, Myanmar and Taiwan; and Korea with Indonesia, Mongolia, the Philippines, Sri Lanka, Thailand and Vietnam. In spite of bilateral agreements, there are still problems of monitoring, enforcement and the lack of redress mechanisms in the host countries. Besides, bilateral ties tend to be weak owing to the lack of regional frameworks to protect migrant rights (Chia 2008).

While many Asian countries have adopted the Universal Declaration of Human Rights, as evidenced by the fact that they have set up national human rights institutions (Office of the High Commissioner for Human Rights 2010), there have been reservations in ratifying the Covenants that have come out of the Declaration targeted at specific groups. One such Covenant is the international instrument protecting the rights of migrants.

The establishment of the 1990 International Convention on the Protection of the Rights of All Migrant Workers and Members of Their Families (otherwise known as the Migrant Worker Convention) is a testimony to the commitment of the United Nations to protect the rights of migrants. In particular, the Convention has been regarded as a significant step forward in migrant protection since earlier covenants only partially addressed the rights violations of migrants. Coming into force in 2003, this legal instrument provides basic provisions to protect the human rights of migrants, especially migrant workers and members of their families (United Nations Educational, Scientific and Cultural Organization 2010). The establishment of the Covenant was aimed at complementing the pioneering efforts of the International Labour Organization (ILO) by way of the Migration for Employment Convention (1949) which grants equal treatment to nationals and non-nationals in the social security field and the protection of acquired rights, and the Migrant Workers (Supplementary Provisions) Convention no. 143 of 1975, which deals with violations of the human rights of migrant workers (Office of the United Nations High Commissioner for Human Rights 1996–2007b).

While incorporating existing non-binding and legally binding UN instruments such as the Universal Declaration of Human Rights and the International Convention on the Elimination of All Forms of Racial Discrimination (ICERD), a basic thrust of the Covenant is that it assumes migrants are social beings and not merely rational economic actors capable of agency and decision-making; for this reason, the Covenant has provisions to protect the families of migrant workers as well, although many migrants, particularly those who are low-skilled, do not have the privilege of taking their families with them into the countries of employment (Fitzpatrick and Kelly 1998–1999).

Currently, international human rights law recognizes an individual's right to leave one's home country but there is the absence of a corresponding right to enter another country without that state's permission (Grant 2005b). Owing to the restrictions placed on the movement and freedom of migrants, an underlying assumption of the Covenant is that it views the migrant through the lens of victimization and, as such, recognizes the vulnerability of migrants. For this reason, the Covenant reaffirms the basic rights of all migrant workers and members of their families, notably the right to life, the right to leave any state including the state of origin, and the right to liberty of movement in the state of employment (United Nations Educational, Scientific and Cultural Organization 2010).

Several articles in the Convention protect migrants from exploitation and abuse against slavery and servitude and from violence, physical injury, threats and intimidation although none appear to address women migrants' vulnerability to sex work and sexual abuse (Fitzpatrick and Kelly 1998–1999). Furthermore, this legal instrument contains provisions to ensure that migrant workers have equal treatment to nationals in the host country in terms of remuneration, hours of work, overtime work, social security, safety, minimum age of employment, and access to housing, social and health services and so forth (Office of the United Nations High Commissioner for Human Rights 1996–2007a).

Similar to the 1951 Convention Relating to the Status of Refugees, Article 1(A)2 recognizes the vulnerability of the migrant, but in this case an individual who is unable to receive protection in his/her own state (Convention and Protocol Relating to the Status of Refugees 2007); the Migrant Worker Convention, in contrast, assumes the vulnerability of the migrant in the receiving state as well. Hence, the Convention assumes that once a state receives a non-national into its territory, the national government has the responsibility of protecting the rights of the migrant (Grant 2005a). In this respect, the Convention goes one step further by protecting the rights of irregular migrants. Should the migrant enter a country in violation of the host's country's immigration laws, this act does not deprive the individual of his/her fundamental human rights, nor does it nullify the responsibility of the host country to protect the migrant. The Convention, thus, calls upon states to protect the fundamental rights of migrant workers irrespective of the immigrant status of the migrant.

Unlike the other international human rights legislations targeted at migrants such as refugees handled by UNHCR's mandate and the labour rights of migrant workers covered by the ILO treaties, the Migrant Worker Convention has opened up new ways of regulating not only the relationship between the individual and the state irrespective of whether s/he is a citizen of that state, but also the 'social conditions that figure so prominently in individual and group migration decisions' (Schuck 2000: 190).

In Asia, states that have become signatories to the Convention are: Bangladesh, Cambodia and Indonesia; states that have ratified the Convention are: the Philippines, Sri Lanka and Timor-Leste (United Nations Treaty Collection 2010a). Of the labour-receiving countries in Asia, none have signed the Migrant Worker Convention, indicating the limits of this instrument to protect migrant rights (International Women's Rights Action Watch Asia Pacific *et al.* 2009; Oishi 2005; Pécoud 2009). An explanation put forward for the reluctance of states to sign the Convention is that they do not wish to extend protection to irregular workers, as required by the Convention (Grant 2005b). Interestingly, this follows the international trend where it was found that only 40 countries have signed the Convention, none of which has been a major migrant labour-receiving country, thereby largely signalling the ineffectiveness of this international legal instrument (Cholewinski *et al.* 2009). In fact in Asia, significant differences in response between labour-sending and labour-receiving countries toward the Convention have been noted: the human rights approach has been received with greater ease in the sending countries; by contrast in the receiving countries, the term 'human rights' has been variously interpreted according to local definitions of civil liberties. As such, these countries have been found to 'lack . . . political will' to enforce the protection of migrant rights and, subsequently, have not ratified the international instruments related to migrant workers (Oishi 2005; Piper 2004b: 71).

In order to promote the Convention among states, within the UN, a Working Group of Intergovernmental Experts on the Human Rights of Migrants was set up in 1997 by the UN Human Rights Commission, leading to the appointment of a Special Rapporteur on Human Rights of Migrants in 1999 (Pécoud and de Guchteneire 2004). As a result of this appointment, a Global Campaign for the ratification of the Migrant Worker Convention was launched in 1998, harnessing the efforts of international organizations and non-governmental organizations with the aim of encouraging states to sign this Convention. This effort had some impact on the ground with the number of signatories increasing from 7 to 12 and ratifications from 9 to 20 (Oishi 2005). In Asia, the Global Campaign had the positive outcome of drawing two countries, namely Bangladesh and Cambodia, into the fold of becoming signatories to the Convention. The Philippines and Sri Lanka were exceptional, having ratified the Convention in July 1995 and March 1996 respectively (United Nations Treaty Collection 2010a).

That only a handful of states in Asia have signed the Convention indicates that there continues to be a reluctance to ratify this international law, clearly signifying the tension over how states wish to express their sovereignty in the granting of migrants their rights. In fact, it was found that the ratification rate of this Convention is low especially among the labour-receiving countries compared with the other treaties such as CEDAW (United Nations Treaty Collection 2010b), signalling the worsening trend in the protection of human rights in particular to migrants (Pécoud and de Guchteneire 2004).

For this reason, there have been discussions to link the Migrant Worker Convention to CEDAW with the aim of pushing countries to ratify the former Convention. In fact, this approach mirrors earlier arguments put forth that a panoply of human rights treaties should be considered in upholding migrant rights, aside from the Migrant Worker Convention alone since the latter has 'limitation[s] on the obligations that states owe to women migrants' (Satterthwaite 2005: 1). Although this seems like a promising approach since all 10 Association of Southeast Asian Nation (ASEAN) countries are signatories to CEDAW, it is still to be seen if this would be an effective strategy to promote the protection of migrant rights. In addition, because CEDAW is a women's bill of rights, it is more likely that women's migrant rights more than men's migrant rights would be protected if this strategy were to be adopted. Furthermore, there is evidence to show that there continues to be obstacles to the full implementation of CEDAW, thereby indicating that migrant rights may not be necessarily protected as assumed (International Women's Rights Action Watch Asia Pacific *et al.* 2009).

Given these trends in the region, the ambivalence of states towards the human rights discourse both in law and governance has been an underlying factor in the persistence of migrant rights abuses in Asia (Devasahayam 2006a). It cannot be denied that states are ambivalent towards the Convention because of the refusal to equate the rights and entitlements of migrant workers to that of local citizens, as this would mean having to apply the notions of citizenship to a migrant and, by extension, the entitlements granted to a citizen (Turner 1993).

Some scholars have argued that the conventional definition of citizenship linking the individual to a bundle of rights and duties by virtue of membership to a political community no longer has the import it once had because of globalization (Held 1999). Arguments have been made that globalization has 'weaken[ed the] traditional bonds of identity between individuals and the state' (Falk 2000: 5) and that nationalism need not be predicated on notions of the society and the nation-state as a discrete, bounded entity (Beck 2000). Brodie (2004: 325) makes a similar point by saying that inevitably human rights have to be central to the concept of the transnational subject since the latter presupposes that 'the fundamental right of all individuals to non-discrimination as well as their social, economic and political needs surpass the sovereignty of national states'.

This line of argument contests the strict dichotomy between human rights and citizen rights where the former is considered 'innate and inalienable' while the latter is 'created by states' (Isin and Turner 2008: 12). In fact, it is exactly the nexus between the concepts related to transnationality and human rights that forms the bedrock of the Migrant Worker Convention. An assumption in the Convention is that migrants have 'multiple citizenship' (Castles and Davidson 2000) in that they possess rights, duties and entitlements in the states of employment as much as they do in the states of origin – an assumption that has been rejected by many receiving countries in the world as well as in Asia, leaving millions of migrant workers vulnerable to a multitude of abuses.

In many receiving countries in Asia, however, there is an exercise of political patronage for skilled workers whose rights are protected through the granting of a wide array of privileges principally to attract them to stay. The perception of low-skilled workers differs markedly. Labour migration policies for this group tend to place limits on: migration, the duration of migration, and integration into the local population by migrants (Piper 2004b).

Related to this, governments of receiving countries are of the opinion that because the presence of low-skilled migrants is transient, hence their needs are a non-issue. In the receiving country of Singapore, for example, migrant workers have been politically and socially constructed on a 'use and discard' basis (Yeoh and Huang 2000: 416–17) because, as Vedi Hadiz reiterates: 'migrant workers are perceived to be of a different nationality and background and in a subordinate class position in society, which means you can do anything you want with them' (Yeo 2004: 3) and, therefore, it is acceptable to deny them their basic human rights. By reinforcing the 'otherness' of this group, receiving countries have distanced themselves from being inclusive and, in turn, failed to uphold contemporary notions of citizenship (Bosniak 2002).

While transnational employment for migrants opens up opportunities for improvement for one's family, migrant workers are vulnerable to a range of abuses over which they have very little control. This chapter posits that while men migrants face difficulties in the migration process, women migrants face greater labour abuses because of the kind of work they take on (Huang and Yeoh 2003). And because the kind of work men and women migrants find abroad tends to be demarcated along gender differences, concomitantly there is a gender dimension to the lack of access to rights protection, particularly among women migrant workers.

That migrant workers represent a 'temporary' feature in the labour landscape of the receiving countries in Asia is not the main factor for their rights abuse, as argued in this chapter. The assertion here instead is that it is the nature of work women migrants take on that increases their vulnerability to human rights violations – work that is connected to women's caring and nurturing roles and, therefore, considered non-work and peripheral to the formal economy. Thus for unskilled women migrants, undertaking work that demands emotional labour throws up complex situations of opportunity and risk.

Migrating for work: are there gendered trends in labour abuses?

Of the world's total population of migrants, Asia and the Pacific is host to more than 50 million migrants (United Nations Economic and Social Commission for Asia and the Pacific 2008). In the region, international migration for low-skilled migrants fills labour shortage gaps in agriculture, the construction, labour-intensive manufacturing, ship-building and cleaning industries. In the receiving countries, certain kinds of jobs have become known as migrants' jobs since they are no longer filled by the local labour force (United Nations Economic and Social Commission for Asia and the Pacific 2008). Among both men and women migrants in Asia, international migration presupposes that the kind of work they take on tends to be temporary, employed on work permits and, thus, differentiated from skilled migrants. Rights abuses, however, tend to be more rampant among low-skilled workers than skilled migrants because the latter group tends to be granted rights akin to permanent residents or even citizens of the state.

By and large, both male and female low-skilled migrant workers in the region tend not to have an adequate understanding and knowledge of the full scope of the dangers, risks and problems they may face in the migration process. In addition, many are not aware of the legal institutional channels they should seek for safe migration, nor the rights and obligations of the working contract and the situation and conditions of work in the host country (Devasahayam 2010). Currently in some sending countries, there exist labour policies and programmes to ensure that migrants utilize safe migration channels so as to reduce the abuses faced by migrant workers. But many of these policies and programmes tend to focus on labour placement rather than labour protection, thereby having little effect on minimizing the abuses migrants encounter.

Among low-skilled migrant workers, there is the recognition that most rights abuses begin in the sending country. This is not to say that problems are not generated in the host country. It is usually in the host country that the problems migrants face in their home countries become manifest or heightened. The first and obvious source of abuse is the recruitment agents operating in the sending countries. These recruitment agents who go out to the villages with the aim of 'recruiting' workers have been found to siphon off huge sums of money in exchange for securing employment prospects for potential migrants. Often these recruitment agents justify the fees they charge, claiming that the money collected goes toward processing the necessary paperwork for the potential migrant's employment abroad and their passport, and the airfare; among potential women migrants, recruitment agents purport that the fees they require are channelled into the training a woman migrant must undergo in preparation for the kind of work she will take on in the receiving country. Unfortunately because many potential migrant men and women are ignorant of the formal migration processes involved in taking up employment in the host country, many are highly dependent on unscrupulous agents who take advantage of their vulnerability.

Another abuse is that low-skilled migrants are banned from employment in destination economies should they be found to be HIV positive. Deportation both for men and women migrant workers who have been found to be HIV positive has been the labour practice of many receiving countries in the region. The non-governmental organization, Coordination of Action Research on AIDS and Mobility (CARAM Asia) has consistently taken the position that subjecting migrant workers to the HIV tests is a discriminatory practice which violates the rights of migrant workers since it causes displacement and puts an end to opportunities to generate income for the affected individuals. But their campaigns have had little effect on the policies of receiving countries. Those migrants found to be HIV positive are often stigmatized and discriminated (United Nations Development Programme 2008). Also migrant workers who are deported risk being in poorer health and suffer a decline in well-being because of the absence of reintegration programmes by host countries (ibid.). Moreover, many potential or current migrants are forced to sign a consent form and are rarely informed what they are being tested for. Furthermore, pre- and post-test counselling are usually not provided for them, which in effect violates international standards set out by UNAIDS (The Joint United Nations Programme on HIV/AIDS) (Coordination of Action Research on AIDS and Mobility (CARAM Asia) 2006).

Working in conditions of servitude is not uncommon for both men and women migrant workers. In Malaysia, those who flee from abusive labour conditions run the risk of becoming illegal migrants and consequently are subject to arrest, imprisonment, caning and deportation (*Newsweek*, 24 March 2008). Abuse also occurs when the employer withholds the migrant worker's passport or salary. Often employers guilty of such abuses are not prosecuted until the abuse is raised with the relevant authorities. Because work conditions related to wages, rest days, medical benefits and so forth are negotiated between the employer and migrant worker, this leaves the migrant worker open to abuse if the employer does not keep his/her part of the bargain.

But low-skilled male migrant workers have been found to possess an advantage over low-skilled women migrants in one respect. For example, in Singapore, male migrants do not face the extent of abuses women migrant workers face because the construction sector has become well regulated and supervised by the state (Rahman and Lian 2005). In contrast, female unskilled migrant workers are more vulnerable to degrading labour practices. Besides being paid much lower wages than men migrant workers (Kaur 2007), their low class status has been found to be reinforced, for example, in the way these workers are commodified: photographs of these women dressed in their work uniforms and holding various household appliances are displayed in the windows of many recruitment agents' offices. Although this practice has been touted as demeaning to women by a Ministry of Manpower, Singapore official, it has never ceased, testifying to how the Singaporean public continues to view this group (*The Straits Times*, 15 October 2003).

Besides, protest against abuse is not unheard of among men migrant workers. In 2004, over 150 Indian migrant workers protested because their employer had failed to pay them their salaries (Think Centre, 17 July 2004). In this case, their protest was not only heard but brought about some resolution; the workers were sent home with compensation from the government but much less than they were promised by their employers. The government's response was that wage claims are usually resolved unless the company for which the migrant worker worked has been liquidated (*The Straits Times*, Forum, 20 January 2009). Protests from men migrants appear to be acceptable in authoritarian Singapore possibly because men migrant workers are by law permitted to join unions to voice their grievances. This has not been the experience of women migrants (Asian Human Rights Commission 2001). Similar protests by women migrants have not occurred in Malaysia, Taiwan and countries in the Middle East and Gulf States except in Hong Kong where their concerns are often framed as global, transnational and human rights rather than local worker rights (Constable 2009). Because of fewer legal and institutional mechanisms to resolve the labour problems they face, women migrants more than men migrants, thus, tend to face greater vulnerabilities.

When care work is not considered 'real' work

> We have launched a campaign to recognize domestic workers as workers. Immediately there is a need to give a paid day off to all domestic workers and a standardized contract that will clearly state the terms and conditions of employment. The Human Resources Ministry can no longer remain silent as it is part of the abuse and exploitation of domestic workers. The Ministry must do justice to more than half a million women who are working as domestic workers in this country.
>
> (Fernandez n.d.)

Campaigns to recognize care work as 'real' work have been ongoing across the labour-receiving countries. Non-governmental organizations assert that because care work is rarely treated as real work, domestic workers are not recognized as workers in an economically productive sense and, therefore, are not protected through effective legislation. The case of Singapore is a notable example aside from Malaysia, as the above quote depicts. In Singapore, migrant women working as foreign domestic workers do not come under the protection of the Employment Act, applicable to the majority of workers in Singapore. In the past, the Singapore government has asserted that it is impractical to have domestic workers covered by the Employment Act because it is impossible to regulate working hours and hours of rest. Furthermore, they have maintained that it is difficult to enforce work conditions in the privacy of a home and when routines in a home vary.

'Behind closed doors': the persistence of rights violations

Because care work is relegated to low status, the work is associated with a string of rights abuses. It has been well documented that the nature of the work engaged in by women migrants place them in a vulnerable position to labour abuses (Yeoh *et al.* 2004). There is no doubt that the nature of domestic work that confines women to the private quarters of their employers has led to their 'invisibility', thereby reinforcing their vulnerability (Toyota 2004). Given the nature of domestic work, for example, and that it is carried out in the private domain means that women migrants are open to an array of mental, verbal, physical and sexual abuses with limited access to escape and at times leading to death. Periodically cases of rights abuse have surfaced in the media. The following is one such case:

> Home-maker Yim Pek Ha was found guilty today of grievously hurting domestic helper Nirmala Bonat and sentenced to 18 years in jail . . . The verdict comes after 110 days of proceedings held over four and a half years . . . Yim was charged with four counts of voluntarily causing grievous hurt to the Indonesian, then 19, with a hot iron twice on a day in January and in April 2004, with using hot water on a day in March 2004, and using a metal cup at about 3pm on May 17, 2004 . . . Nirmala's case created an uproar among

Malaysians and Indonesians . . . In Indonesia, it sparked street protests in front of the Malaysian embassy with the people calling for better treatment for domestic helpers.

('Maid abuse: Housewife gets 18 years', *Malaysiakini*,
as cited in Tenaganita 27 November 2008)

In such reported cases, the perpetrator is usually charged according to the laws of the receiving countries. But in reality, most abuses go unchecked since few workers report the abuse they encounter because they lack information on who to turn to for help.

Reports from Lebanon show that at least six domestic workers were forced into suicide because of poor working conditions and employer abuse. While it is common for passports to be withheld, it is also not uncommon for these women to be locked away for years by employers who do not allow them to leave the home. The Philippines has installed a ban on its women taking on employment in Lebanon because of the rising suspicious deaths among domestic workers (*Asian Migration News*, 1–30 November 2009). Nepal has followed suit following the death of two Nepali women in late November in 2009.

There is growing awareness of the isolation and vulnerability of these women to labour exploitation and violence in some countries, such as in Thailand where there are more than 100,000 women from Myanmar alone who are employed as domestic workers (Toyota 2004). Unlike men migrants, women migrants are at risk of being vulnerable to sexual abuse because of their gender identity. While the majority of domestic workers are fortunate to work in a safe environment, yet there are some who are vulnerable to sexual abuse (Yeoh *et al.* 2004). Of the 528 domestic workers who participated in Mahidol University's IPSR study in 2002–2003, one in ten of them mentioned being forced to submit to physical abuse with almost 20 per cent reporting that they were touched without their approval; 8 per cent encountering sexual advances; and 1.3 per cent falling victim to rape (Huguet and Punpuing 2005). In some cases, should an unplanned pregnancy result, the woman migrant usually ends up being deported unless she is able to report the case to the relevant authorities.

Because of the stark rise in domestic worker abuses in Singapore in the 1990s, the government amended its Penal Code to prosecute perpetrators of 'maid abuse' in the country. While errant employers found abusing their foreign workers are liable to be prosecuted in court and punished by law, recent amendments to the Penal Code have had the effect of placing heavier penalties – such as fines, imprisonment and even caning – on employers, if found guilty. Moreover, guilty employers and their spouses will be blacklisted and permanently barred from employing a foreign worker in the future. Little, however, has been put in place by way of legal mechanisms to deter these acts from occurring in the first place.

Clearly, the amendment and Singapore's judiciary 'represent important safety nets against the abuse of foreign domestic workers . . . [However] the strong arm of the law itself has its limits, as it is often aimed at making employers who commit abusive acts accountable for their actions only after the fact' (Yeoh *et al.*

2004: 20). On the positive side, since maid abuse has come under the public eye through the courts and media, some doctors have been more alert in determining if a domestic worker who undergoes the mandatory bi-annual health examination has been a victim of domestic abuse. The appearance of even a slight bruise on the body of a domestic worker can set off alarms, as reported by some domestic workers. This health surveillance technique has been adopted by some in the medical community.

Where are the rights of migrant women?

Because work contracts fail to stipulate the number of hours of work, many women migrants who work as foreign domestic workers risk working longer hours than expected compared with workers in other labour sectors. This violation of their worker rights has been found to have debilitating health outcomes for them. In a study conducted by the Institute of Health Policy and Management of the College of Public Health, National Taiwan University, domestic workers reported working an average of 13 hours a day while struggling with muscular-skeletal discomforts, menstrual pain, headaches, and irritable stomachs (Cheng and Chen 2006). Particularly Indonesian women complained about exhaustion from overwork as they were forced to help out in their employers' businesses during the day while engaging in domestic work at night.

Experiencing work overload meant that these women suffered from greater physical fatigue which left them vulnerable to a range of medical complications. While the lack of sleep and physical fatigue were the health-related problems that were often cited by domestic workers, these workers also suffered mental stress. A study of 290 Filipina domestic workers in Hong Kong revealed that mental stress was also expressed in the following behaviours: waking up in the early hours of the day, loneliness, worry and encountering difficulties in sleeping (Holroyd *et al.* 2001).

(De)sexualizing women migrants

Migrants have been found to be in reasonably good health possibly as an outcome of migration being a selective process that weeds out the unhealthy from the healthy. Hence, the term 'healthy migrant effect' came into existence (Aiyer *et al.* 2004; cf. Fernail 2005; Sundquist 2001: 691). Nevertheless, women migrants encounter discrimination in that they are denied access to certain healthcare services available to the local population. Governments of many receiving countries block women migrants' access to certain healthcare services as a way of reinscribing their temporary status and socially differentiating them from the local population (Devasahayam 2006b). Sexual and reproductive health is one major area in which women migrants face discrimination. In this case, migration accentuates the socio-economic differences of the two populations, leading to potential discrepancies in health outcomes to emerge between the host and migrant communities (Aiyer *et al.* 2004; Jatrana *et al.* 2005).

In Malaysia and Singapore, for example, employment rules for women migrants reflect an ideology of oppression when labour regulations demand an 'a-sexual' woman migrant worker. In this regard, domestic workers employed in Singapore are stripped of their rights to undergo any form of marriage, or apply to marry, under any law, religion, custom or usage, a Singaporean citizen or Permanent Resident (Devasahayam 2010). Related to this, a woman migrant is prohibited from becoming pregnant or delivering a child in Singapore during the validity of her work permit. Moreover, these women are not granted access to reproductive health services in the countries of employment. In Singapore, a woman migrant's rights are further curtailed when her employer ends up policing her sexual behaviour for fear of losing the security bond of Singapore $5,000 if the woman migrant is found to be pregnant based on the results of the 6 monthly medical examination (Devasahayam 2010). But in reality, if she is found to be pregnant, the employer does not lose the security bond as long as the domestic worker is repatriated within a week to her home country.

The exercise of reproductive health rights, however, varies across the Southeast Asian region depending on locality. Burmese domestic workers in Thailand have a different experience because there are no legal measures barring them from being sexually active during their employment in Thailand. This does not mean that their reproductive health rights are completely protected. Instead domestic workers who were interviewed in a study said that their main primary health concerns included their lack of access to birth control, safe abortion, and pre- and post-natal care and adequate information about the various birth control methods and their side effects (Panam *et al*. 2005). Among those who want to end their pregnancies, they either sought the help of a traditional Burmese or Thai midwife or birth attendants because abortion is illegal. This, however, often leads to medical complications, thus subjecting these women to various health risks (Panam *et al*. 2005).

Other health-related rights violations

Although employment laws and regulations in the Asian region serve to supervise the migratory trajectories of women migrants, they never fully facilitate the rights of migrant workers to their basic needs. In many receiving countries, health outcomes among women migrants are linked to whether she is made to feel as 'a family member, an employee, or a slave' (Chang and Groves 2000: 77), with greater integration into the family signalling a higher probability of being taken care of including in matters of health. In many instances, however, a woman migrant is unable to exercise her own right to seek medical counsel if she so wishes because she does not have the necessary identification since it is common practice for employers to retain their passports. Clearly this situation creates a dependency relationship between the employer and domestic worker with the employer determining her worker's access to medical care.

That employers may assert their hegemony over domestic workers was observed among Burmese migrant workers in Thailand whose employers, in many cases, determined the severity of the illness and how the woman migrant should go about seeking medical treatment. It is for this reason many women migrants usually obtained the permission of their employers before they sought help from a health professional. In cases of abused workers, the situation is less than ideal because denial of access to healthcare by a person in authority reinforces the unequal power relations between employer and worker. Furthermore, the domestic worker faces an increased risk of suffering from irreversible health effects.

Studies on health rights in various receiving destinations, however, produced contrasting evidence. In Singapore, some domestic workers have been reported to freely relegate their decision-making powers to their employers. Migrant women of Sri Lankan and Tamil descent often agreed to have their employers keep their documents as well as accompany them to the doctor as they spoke about being afraid of seeking help themselves. In the same country, Filipinos provided a contrast as they preferred to see to their health needs themselves, perceiving it to be a personal or private concern.

Whether a migrant woman chooses to exercise her health rights depends largely on the nature of her relationship with her employer. The fear of losing one's job was a commonly cited reason for not seeking healthcare assistance. Panam *et al.* (2005) reported this for Burmese domestic workers in Thailand who stated they did not want to miss work for a few days as a result of an illness for fear of aggravating their employers. Curiously, Holroyd *et al.* (2001) found a similar response from Filipina domestic workers in Hong Kong in spite of assumptions that this group may be more aware of their worker rights, given that they have effectively organized themselves into unions (International Labour Organization 1998). In addition, domestic workers were afraid that their employers would deduct wages for any sick days taken and, hence, would rather continue working in spite of being ill (Huguet and Punpuing 2005). Particularly among domestic workers who feel that work opportunities are difficult to secure and who feel the pressing need to continue in their jobs for financial reasons, they are left with little choice but to 'conceal' their illness rather than assert their rights (Toyota 2004).

Trafficked for sex 'work': conditions and solutions

In Asia, seeking wage work among poor women has been complicated by human trafficking. Nearly one-third of the global trafficking trade includes women and children from Southeast Asia, the majority of whom tend to be trafficked to other countries in the region. Some sources have estimated that 200,000–250,000 women and children from the region are trafficked annually (International Organization for Migration 2000). In Southeast Asia, concern about human trafficking has intensified since the 1980s because of the thriving sex trade, child prostitution, and the spread of HIV. Invariably, trafficking has been associated with sex work, migration through undocumented channels, criminality, labour exploitation, and the violation of human rights.

Human trafficking is a growing concern in the region because of the large waves of mobility especially among low-skilled women within and across countries (Gallagher 2005). These women are particularly vulnerable to becoming victims of trafficking because of the lack of adequate social and human capital. Among them, poverty creates vulnerability to trafficking because of the temptation to travel abroad with strangers, even without proper documentation, on the promise of prospective employment in foreign countries. Research also shows that conditions in their families such as domestic violence, the need to escape from household problems and family dissolution are critical push factors (Yea 2005).

The link between undocumented migration and trafficking in persons has been well established. The 2008 Regional Thematic Working Group on International Migration in East and South-East Asia report reveals that the vulnerability to exploitation and abuse increases because of the irregular status of the migrants (International Organization for Migration 2008). In these cases, the rights of these women migrants are severely compromised. Particularly undocumented women migrants, who have been promised employment in the domestic work sector, have found themselves being 'victims of illegal placement by recruitment agencies' and forced into sex work instead on arrival in the receiving country (Komnas Perempuan *et al.* 2006: 25). According to an Indonesian country report to the UN Special Rapporteur on the Human Rights of Migrants submitted in 2003, many housemaid agencies have been used as a 'cover' for the trafficking of women for sex work and 'in this context, the existence and operations of recruitment agencies are part and parcel of the chain of transboundary organized crime' (ibid. : 24).

In Southeast Asia, Malaysia and Thailand have been found to have large numbers of undocumented migrant workers. 2005 saw an estimated 1.1 million undocumented workers in Thailand alone coming mainly from Cambodia, Laos and Myanmar (International Organization for Migration 2008). Because of the vulnerability to abuse experienced by undocumented migrants, on the adoption of the Migrant Workers Convention in 1990, the Summit called for governments to cooperate in reducing the cause of undocumented migration and in prosecuting criminals engaged in the organization of the trafficking in human beings, 'while safeguarding the basic human rights of undocumented migrants, preventing their exploitation, and offering them appropriate means of appeal in accordance with national legislation' (Fact Sheet No. 24, The Rights of Migrant Workers 1990).

It has long been recognized that the problem of trafficking in persons can only be addressed by concrete measures at various levels. Because human trafficking is a transnational crime, a transnational response was unanimously agreed upon, favouring the enforcement of the United Nations Protocol to Prevent, Suppress and Punish Trafficking in Persons, Especially Women and Children (UN Protocol on Trafficking), the most comprehensive anti-trafficking instrument in international law, in 2003. Countries have also come up with action plans to solve the problem. The Indonesian government has in place a National Action Plan against Trafficking to draft an anti-trafficking bill (Komnas Perempuan *et al.* 2006). Other counter-trafficking initiatives include prevention through laws and the judicial system; protection for victims of trafficking; and the return and reintegration of victims to their home countries.

While the legal frameworks to combat trafficking regionally in Southeast Asia are paramount, it has been argued that the countries comprising the Association of Southeast Asian Nations (ASEAN) have 'failed to deal with the problem effectively' by penalizing the trafficking act rather than 'address[ing] the socio-economic causes and consequences of sex trafficking' (Cheah 2006: 47). As such, women who are trafficked continue to be blamed for the crime. In Malaysia, trafficked victims as well as migrants whose employers have committed labour rights violations have been found to be prosecuted under the country's immigration laws instead of being rendered assistance. It was discovered by Suhakam, the national Human Rights Commission, that many foreign women in Malaysia's prisons are in fact trafficked victims (Human Rights Watch, 18 May 2005).

Conclusion

In spite of women migrants facing difficult working conditions, poor remuneration and constant surveillance by both the state and their employers, many continue to choose to work abroad because of the perceived benefits (Chin 1998; Heyzer 1986; Huang and Yeoh 1996). While the majority of low-skilled migrants leave their countries for work abroad through documented channels, many use undocumented and, therefore, unsafe migration routes and, as such, become vulnerable to various abuses. But it must be emphasized that the migration experience of those who take the safe migration route need not be entirely devoid of problems since the rights of these individuals have also been repeatedly violated. For this reason, guaranteeing the rights of all migrant workers becomes paramount because it upholds 'a moral framework of justice and universal human rights based on human functions or capabilities such as the ability to live a normal life expectancy and be free from assault' (Turner 2005: 408).

Currently, labour policies concerning women migrants in many receiving countries in Asia tend to be discriminatory as they deny migrant women the rights accorded to nationals. Their strict laws are in keeping with many theories of citizenship: that states will use whatever power it has to monitor, control and restrict the immigration of nationals from another country (Koslowski 2000). The exercise of citizenship in this case is about exclusion or 'social closure', to appropriate a term coined by Rogers Brubaker (1992: 21–34), arguably essential to the systemic stability of countries. Such an approach is also discriminatory in another way – it reinforces the gender, class, and race/ethnic identities of women migrant workers, beyond reinforcing citizenship disparities (cf. Sen 1994). In the long run, however, these rules cannot be justified especially when the rights of transient groups in the receiving country may have repercussions on the local population.

For the thousands of women migrants, thus, the stakes are high since they are left with little protection by the relevant international Covenants and bilateral frameworks. As a result, non-governmental organizations and faith-based organizations have sprouted all across the world in response to the needs of this labour group (Ball and Piper 2002; Gurowitz 1999, 2000; Law 2003; Law and Nadeau 1999; Mackie 2001; Piper 2003), especially when embassies and states have failed to look into the welfare of these women (United Nations Development Programme 2008). International and civil society organizations have repeatedly reiterated the necessity and urgency of protecting the rights of migrants at the national and transnational levels. Their point of departure has been that protecting the rights of migrants enables these individuals to contribute fully to the development process whether of the host and home countries but also of the individuals themselves (Global Migration Group 2008).

Ensuring the rights of migrants means that governments of sending, transit and receiving countries are responsible for embracing the rights approach in the enforcement of national labour laws, policies and practices, as well as ratifying the international treaties for migrant protection. While the advocacy efforts of these organizations have the 'great potential to bridge the difficult nexus between citizenship and human rights' by 'linking to transnational networks and campaigns' (Piper 2003: 741), to date, most of these organizations have achieved limited success, indicating how women migrants as a group continue to be construed by governments in the countries of employment (Piper 2004b). Besides, as long as care work is socially constructed as peripheral to the formal economy, it can be expected that granting greater protection to these women will not be a priority in most receiving countries in the years to come.

5   Women executives and emotional labour

The work–life balance of professional women in the Asia-Pacific and the US

Ann Brooks

Introduction

Globalization is fundamentally restructuring traditional labour markets and the way in which individuals are redefining their market position and their work–life balance. There has been virtually no research on how specific pressures of the global economy affect the prospects for care-giving among highly skilled, well-heeled, First World professionals (Blair-Loy and Jacobs 2003). These high-end 'servants of globalization' (Salazar Parreñas 2001a) face a range of new pressures from increased competition, workplace and time pressures. McDowell (1997) has shown how international banks and corporations are providing a range of in-house services for employees, but the responsibility of much caregiving and emotional labour remains the responsibility of the employee and is likely to be associated with greater dependence on paid caregiving.

High-ranking professional women, like their male colleagues, face workplace cultures that assume elite employees will put in very long hours on an interrupted and full-time basis, even during the family formative years (Epstein *et al.* 1999; Williams 2000). This chapter reviews the position of professional women in a range of occupations and domestic contexts and assesses the impact of emotional labour demands on their careers and their work–life balance. This chapter draws on research from the US and Asia.

Globalization and the concentration of key economic functions and resources in global cities have resulted in the growth of a transnational professional class of workers. The demand for high-level professional workers globally has led to more women moving into the upper levels of corporate and other professional jobs (Sassen 2003). Despite the global recession, women's recruitment into these areas is likely to continue, if not significantly expand. The reason for this, as Sassen (ibid.: 310) observes, is that 'women are seen rightly or wrongly, as better cultural brokers, and these skills matter to global firms. In the financial-services industry, women are considered crucial to interfacing with consumers, because they are believed to inspire more trust' (see Fisher 2002).

Marchand and Runyan (2000) claim that the impact of the new economy is diverse and has material and political implications. The global economy often reinforced in state discourses positions women in an ambiguous and contradictory position in regard to economic discourses and public policies. As Marchand and Runyan (ibid.: 15) comment:

> [I]n the US women are caught between the neo-liberal rhetoric which casts women as the 'new entrepreneurs' by devolving women's traditional family roles and neo conservative views which emphasize 'family values' and cast women as selfish and irresponsible if they do not fulfil their mothering roles.

It is in this context of the movement of women more fully into professionally demanding occupations that the renewed debate around emotional labour and the commercialization of intimate life has emerged.

Single professionals and two career households prefer urban to suburban residences and, as Sassen (2003) has noted, this has led to an expansion of high-income families and residential areas and a return to family life in urban areas, albeit on a different basis. Thus a new form of social and economic arrangement is seen to characterize family life, whereby, as Sassen notes: 'urban professionals want it all including dogs and children, whether or not they have time to care for them' (ibid.: 258).

There have been wide-ranging debates within society and among parents in the past few years about how to manage emotional labour demands and maintain careers and jobs. Emotional labour demands include the range of caring responsibilities involved in childcare, care of the aged and infirm, and the emotional investment in managing and maintaining a household. There is very clearly a gender imbalance in the allocation of these responsibilities, with women traditionally managing emotional labour demands at the expense of careers.

Some social scientists claim we are experiencing a 'commercialization of intimate life' as both single parents and couples seek to transfer emotional labour demands from the home to professional agencies. The entrance of emotion labour debates into the considerations of work and organizations has occurred alongside other significant developments concerning the growth in the service economy and the 'feminization' of local labour markets. This has led to a greater need to focus on the eliciting of desired emotions in the provision of service and has placed emotion work and emotional labour at the forefront of analysis.

The growth of research into emotional labour and interest in emotional labour has partly resulted from the increase in the number of women and mothers in the labour force. Globally women's engagement in wage work is increasing at a faster rate than men's. In 1993, the International Labour Organization (2003) documented 53.5 per cent of women in the labour force while in 2003 the percentage had increased to 53.9 per cent. Men showed a converse pattern as their participation dropped from 80.5 per cent to 79.4 per cent. In the Asia-Pacific region, the share of women in employment rose from 29 per cent to 31 per cent during the same time span.

Alongside this, the past 10 to 15 years have seen an acceleration in what has been called 'the commercialization of intimate life' (Hochschild, 2003a, 2005). This can be seen in the expansion of caring and other services to support aspects of life traditionally seen as the domain of the family. This is most visible among the affluent middle class but it now permeates all sectors of society.

The figures for mothers and women in employment globally, based on data from the OECD (2002) show the percentage of mothers with at least one child under 6 who work full-time varies from 55.5 per cent in the UK, 61.2 per cent in the US, 46.9 per cent in Italy, 66.2 per cent in Belgium, 69.8 per cent in Portugal, 74.3 per cent in Denmark, 58.6 per cent in France, 66.4 per cent in the Netherlands, 66.0 per cent in Austria and a surprisingly low 45.0 per cent in Australia. There is not space here to discuss some significant variations in these figures, see Brooks (2008b) for a full discussion of the differences in rates and possible reasons for this.

It is clear that neither men's care in couple households nor formal childcare structures are filling the gaps created by women in the workforce. Australia has a 'lower maternal employment rate consistent with more traditional family models' than other industrial nations (OECD 2002; Whitehouse and Hosking 2005; Maher *et al.* 2008). While Australia may not be typical in terms of patterns of caring, it is clear that men are not taking up the 'care deficit' (Pocock 2006) created by women's paid work. Maher *et al.* (2008: 550) provide the following indicators as evidence:

> the persistence of longer hours of employment for men with young children compared with men without children (Whitehouse and Hosking 2005); very low availability and take up of any paternity leave (EOWA 2006) and the predominance of women in the part-time and casualised labour market.

Meeting the emotional labour demands of professional women in the Asia-Pacific and the US

For the middle-class working woman in Asia-Pacific and the US, increased work opportunities for professional women in addition to a range of other demographic factors have put significant pressure on women to look for a range of solutions to parenting and emotional labour demands. Factors which have led to increased pressure on professional women include: demographic factors including an increase in divorce rates and an increase in the number of female-headed single parent families; the changing nature of work and organizations which requires a more internationally mobile workforce; the blurring of the work–life balance which shows women to be worse off across a range of indices measuring the work–life balance; the growth in opportunities for professional women; increased availability and mobility of a domestic service industry; and the demands of dual career families and their impact on emotional labour responsibilities.

Demographic statistics in the US show that the divorce rate in the US is 50 per cent and one-fifth of all households are headed by single women. In addition, most of these mothers get little financial help from their spouses and most of these women work full-time. In the US, statistics show that a third of single mothers never remarry and the two-thirds who do remarry, over half divorce again. The pattern is for single mother to co-habit but the rate of break-up is higher for cohabiting couples, so the burden of emotional labour falls on single mothers. Given the pressures emerging from changing patterns of marriage, divorce and parenting, how are professional women coping with emotional labour demands? We explore this issue in the context of the Asia-Pacific and the US.

Domestic arrangement patterns after divorce can be seen as an example of new gendered patterns of care (Maher *et al.* 2008). In Australia, they note that '[m]en after divorce undertake more domestic labour than any other group of Australian men' (Baxter *et al.* 2007). Additionally, as Qu and Weston (2005) observe, paid work is as critical to family well-being as the provision of hands-on care: 'women's greater access to this form of economic caring, as well as changes to men's labour market participation, may be having complex effects on gendered time within households' (Maher *et al.* 2008: 551). In fact, Broomhill and Sharp (2004) suggest a variety of alternative breadwinner models have emerged, at least in Australia.

The pattern of work, at least until the recent economic recession globally, was following the same pattern in Australia as in the US, rather than in the EU, by deregulating working hours and providing limited family support. It has been noted that with the increases in hours of work and the changes in the standard working week as well as the growth of part-time employment, women's workforce participation has increased in Western economies. However, Maher *et al.* (2008: 552) note: 'This temporal de-regulation in the Australian labour market reforms may represent a gendered double-bind for families seeking to combine work and care.'

Women executives and emotional labour in the US

The relationship between parenting and social class is not a straightforward one when set in the context of practical constraints confronting women in different occupations. As Devasahayam and Yeoh (2007: 8) contend of women executives at the upper end of the occupational hierarchy:

> the dichotomous opposition of work and family is a particularly fraught terrain as they wrestle with the need to excel in both spheres. In contrast it appears that women from lower class groups may experience less intense role conflict integrating the worlds of home and wage work.

Women in executive positions in the US have what Blair-Loy (2003: 204) calls 'ample resources' to address the issues of emotional labour which confront them but face 'formidable structural constraints' because of the demands of a 'focused loyalty' required by higher-level positions. As Blair-Loy notes, these women are constantly straddling worker and mother identities. Women thus find themselves disadvantaged by the demands of some professions and this is then reflected in the reduced number of women rising to senior positions in the company (Blair-Loy 2003; Fuchs Epstein *et al.* 1999; Williams 2000).

Fuchs Epstein *et al.* (1999) found a sharp decrease in the number of women being made partners in law firms after 1990. She found that in the 1990s women were nearly half of the new recruits in top law firms in New York City but

89 per cent of the partners were men. Citing an American Bar Association (ABA) study, it was found that men held 87 per cent of the partners of all law firms and that men were twice as likely to be partners when compared to women of similar background. The same study found that at least 55 per cent of all lawyers worked over 2,400 hours a year. The average law firm in New York City requires associates to bill up to 2,500 hours annually. Williams notes that some firms require billings of 3,000 hours which requires an average of 80 hours in the office a week. Citing the conclusions of an influential report, Williams (2000: 7) notes as follows: 'Legal work makes dramatic demands on the practitioner's time and makes it difficult or nearly impossible to have a life in which family obligations or other non-work activity may be experienced in a conventional way.'

Strategies used by executive women vary depending on resources, cultural context and individual dispositions. Blair-Loy (2003) cites the case of Sarah Jacobs who was recruited as a partner to an entrepreneurial law firm, which was the same year she had a son and shortly before she got divorced. Her resources allowed her to hire a live-in nanny and work very long hours. She comments as follows:

> I knew before I was pregnant that there was never a way I was giving up my career and just sitting at home . . . I couldn't have done it. It wasn't my nature. It wasn't what moved me. This profession gives me in a lot of ways, a real piece of me . . . It's been enormously good for me and not just financially.
>
> (cited in Blair-Loy 2003: 131–2)

Her answer was to buy a condominium near her office and her son's private school rather than live out in the suburbs. Her attitude to mothering is not a 'time intensive mothering situation' but she prioritizes what she sees as important for a quality relationship:

> I never missed a school play . . . Never missed a parent-teacher conference. Never not read a paper before it went through . . . Did I make milk and cookies? I have food in the house. Do all women [who stay home] actually serve dinner? Do I think my kid is suffering for it? Not particularly.

The situation of women in the legal profession is summed up in the case of Rosemary Daszkiewicz, a corporate attorney who writes in the *Washington Bar News* (2002) of the difficulties of maintaining a work–life balance as follows:

> Those who climb the highest rungs are able to put client needs first, no matter how demanding and unyielding – business trips at a moment's notice, dinners, sports and cultural events several times a week, weekends golfing or skiing with clients – not to mention the long hours of work demanded by the economic model we have created. None of this is possible without someone who is available to tend to the children, accommodate their schedules, see to the needs of the extended family, and keep the home in order
>
> (Daszkiewicz 2002: 13, cited in Blair-Loy 2003: 198)

To cope with the competing demands Daszkiewicz works a reduced schedule for lower status and pay, than a full-time partner. She has to struggle to gain the respect of her colleagues because she operates from a part-time position.

In other cases the pressures of mothering have forced women to relinquish their career. Blair-Loy (2003) cites the example of a general manager and president of a successful small company where childbirth did not initially deter her from her career and she was back in the office 6 weeks after giving birth and hired a full-time babysitter. However, she was faced with a dilemma by having to leave on business while her son was recovering from surgery and subsequent to that she moved to a less demanding part-time job.

Blair-Loy (ibid.: 167–8) outlines the kind of dilemma faced by women abandoning full-time vocations, and indicates the struggle women experience in making decisions to give up careers, for example, Jane Rowan who mourned the loss of the respected and glamorous person she had been while she was working as she noted:

> It was like I totally lost my identity. When I was working everyone knew who I was. I was a senior partner in the firm. I had a glamorous career. That defined me. I've got it all, I thought, status, respect. It was a terrible shock to think, I'm nobody now. I'm somebody's mom.

As Blair-Loy (ibid.: 166) comments of a number of instances of women executives across a range of professions: 'the new delegatory model of motherhood remains gendered and hierarchical'. It is very clear that a family's emotional labour remains the responsibility of women when it exceeds what can be purchased. The woman remains the person who shoulders the demands at the expense of her professional career.

Research on career-oriented couples (Blair-Loy 2001, 2003; Blair-Loy and Jacobs 2003; Hochschild 2003a; Williams 2000) highlights the issues confronting both women and men, but particularly women, in demanding positions, who work long hours and who frequently find themselves unsupported by their spouse. Yet as Blair-Loy and Jacobs (2003) note, there has been virtually no research on how specific pressures of the global economy affect emotional labour demands for caregiving among the highly skilled, well-heeled First World professionals (but see Brooks 2006, 2010).

Blair-Loy (2003: 118–19) shows in her study of female executives that two-thirds of the career-committed group responded to these work demands and lack of a caregiving spouse by not having children. As one female executive in an accounting firm commented:

> [The decision not to have kids] was difficult and it took us a long time . . . Someone needed to be available . . . We could certainly afford whatever kind of childcare we would want to have, so that wasn't an issue. But that somebody needed to have flexibility and availability in their schedule. And I wasn't willing to give that up in mine and he wasn't willing to give that up in his . . . So we got a dog (laughter).

The impact of children on women's careers, and the experience of having children for women in senior executive positions, result in a demographic profile highlighting this. Blair-Loy and Jacobs found that among their respondents, men are more likely to have a wife at home or be working part-time, whereas women are either single or married to full-time employed husbands. Seventy-nine per cent of men are married compared to 62 per cent of women, but a much larger percentage of men are likely to have children, 69 per cent compared to 38 per cent. Only five of the female brokers are parents and two of these five women work part-time.

In other cases, career-oriented couples achieved a balance in their professional lives with the help of childcare. Blair-Loy cites the case of a real-estate developer, Anna, who was often absent from home but employed a full-time nanny who cares for their pre-school children. As Blair-Loy (2003: 136) shows, the work pattern they have established is one which is common for many professional couples: 'Anna takes "the early shift" at home before the nanny arrives at 8 am. Her husband is home by the time the nanny leaves at 6.30 pm. Anna often works in the office until late. After dinner, her husband works past midnight in his home office.'

In their study of stockbrokers, Blair-Loy and Jacobs (2003: 235) found that all the female stockbrokers were married and married to husbands who are employed full-time. They note that none of the female brokers has a homemaking spouse or a part-time employed spouse to share the domestic and caregiving responsibilities. Thirty-three per cent of the male brokers have a full-time employed spouse and in these cases there is pressure around caregiving responsibilities (Clarkberg and Moen 2001; Jacobs and Gerson 2001). As one female broker commented: 'I think women have more responsibilities, you know laundry and dinners.' However, some do manage to establish a balance. One female broker-manager manages to spend time with her family in the evening and does her work on her lap-top after her children are in bed. She also spends time working from home at the weekend.

Overall, however, the research conducted by Blair-Loy and Jacobs found that there was a significant caregiving deficit by male brokers. The wives of the stockbrokers said their husbands spent very little time with their families, particularly on childcare and housework. The brokers have a particular perspective as regards caregiving:

> [M]any brokers seem to feel that their responsibility for family care is appropriately limited to leisure related activities on weekends and during short vacations. Most do not seem to view the work of caregiving as a constant ongoing activity for which they have primary responsibility. Several respondents said they relied on weekends as their only time away from the job.
>
> (Blair-Loy and Jacobs 2003: 235)

Female brokers in the survey did far more family caregiving than male brokers. The wives of brokers are encouraged to stay home and to focus on caregiving which enables the male broker to sustain long hours of work and earn a high income. Most brokers say they wanted 'traditional' wives who would stay at home and provide a conventional caregiving role. Some brokers did make some attempt to acknowledge caregiving obligations, as one broker noted, who called himself a 'workaholic' and generally stayed in the office until 8 or 9 pm. He said he achieved work–family balance by moving from the suburbs to a Manhattan apartment near his office so that he could go home after dinner and then return to work at night. This schedule allows him to see his children before they go to bed. This study of stockbrokers appear to have very conventional marriage patterns regarding caregiving and emotional labour. This study and others show that there is little indication of any shift of emotional labour responsibilities to men.

Research on emotional labour in Asia

There has been a wide range of research on female migrant labour in Southeast Asia (Cheng 1996; Chin 1998; Huang and Yeoh 1997; Tan 1999; Wong 1996). Lee (1996) comments that it is indeed ironic that the academic achievements of many women in host countries, for example, professionals in the United States, Canada and Singapore have come through the incorporation of women migrants of minority races as domestic servants and childcare providers. Brooks (2006) notes that highly paid women in academic and corporate life, living and working in Asian cities in Singapore and Hong Kong and having one or two maids, readily admitted that the situation regarding emotional labour obligations would have been far more tense as regards their relationships with their spouse or partner if it had not been for the 'live-in maid'.

Devasahayam and Yeoh (2007) also note that for the middle-class and professional woman in Asia, a live-in domestic worker is indispensable. Devasahayam comments that in countries like Singapore, employing a foreign domestic worker is also a marker of middle-class identity (Chin, 1998). On the indispensability of this paid labour, a Singaporean woman remarked that 'Singapore could no longer do without transnational domestic workers' (Huang *et al.* 2007: 29). Similarly in Vietnam, Bélanger and Oudin (2007) narrate how Vietnamese women who have benefited by a range of economic changes in Vietnam are only able to maintain their economic position because they are able to take advantage of domestic labour. Yarr (1996: 115) in her research found a university professor who said she was only able to cope at home because she had a network of other women who assisted with her emotional labour demands.

One of the reasons for the increase in the growth of female migrant domestic labour is the framing of gender ideology in relation to emotional labour obligations in countries in Asia. National family policies in Malaysia, for example, have consistently emphasized women's role in the family while highlighting their contribution to the economy of the country. Singapore is another case in point, where state policies would have it that women work so as to contribute to the expansion of the economy, yet the dominant ideology posits that women continue to be the primary caretakers of the family.

Stivens (2007) shows that in Malaysia and Singapore the concept of the working woman cannot be divorced from the good mother. Thus the modern woman is synonymous with the working woman. She pursues her career while being a good mother, thus reinforcing family values integral to upholding the moral and social fabric of society. A study by Wong, Yeoh, Graham and Teo (2004) on single fathers in Singapore show that men subscribe to the same values as women, maintaining it was 'unnatural' for men to carry out the nurturer role unlike women who were naturally imbued with 'motherly love'. Single men openly reported wanting to remarry to provide mothers for their children.

A study by Huang, Yeoh and Straughan (2007) found that working women in Southeast Asia make a conscious effort to arrange their travel schedules around their children and often called home to check on the children while on business trips. For these wome, the distance between them and their children did not deter them from carrying on the emotional labour of caring. Professional women were also forced to keep strictly to their busy schedules and return swiftly for the sake of their children. My own research in Hong Kong (Brooks 2006) among academic women found that they were less likely to attend as many academic conferences as their male partners and were more likely to spend the minimum amount of time at a conference. This clearly has an impact on their academic careers.

In the West, women will look to institutional childcare arrangements and part-time work but the experience of Asian women is different, relying on informal childcare arrangements through grandparents or through maids. Policies have supported both with the open-door levy-based policy on migrant domestic labour and the Grandparent Caregiver Tax Relief in Singapore which encourages grandparents as caregivers, and public housing policies which encourage families to live in close proximity.

The stark contrast between Asia and the West can be seen in the case of migrant Chinese academic couples who move to the UK (Cooke 2007). In these cases the wives of highly educated professional men who migrate to the UK from China, who are themselves in professional academic careers find themselves significantly disadvantaged by the patterns of childcare available in the UK. In China, as in other Asian countries, women continue to work full-time during childrearing (Cooke 2007). In fact, as Cooke (ibid.: 49) notes: 'With more than 38 per cent of its full-time workforce being women (*China Statistical Yearbook* 2005) China has one of the highest women's employment participation rates in the world.' Chinese women who migrate with their husbands suffer the disadvantage of being 'trailing wives' in the UK in employment terms and as Cooke (2007: 59) states: 'it is largely women who bear the brunt of anxieties, social isolation, responsibilities and sacrifice' in relation to migration and family life.

'The commercialization of intimate life'

The emphasis of much of the research on emotional labour and the debate about the 'commercialization of intimate life' has come from the US and particularly from the work of Arlie Hochschild (2003a, 2005). Hochschild's groundbreaking work on the concept of emotional labour has provided us with fascinating insights and put the service sector and gender at the heart of our understanding of work in contemporary organizations. As Hochschild (1997) commented in her book *The Managed Heart*: 'the world turns to women for mothering and this fact silently attaches itself to many a job description'. In addition, her work on emotions has facilitated the advance in our understanding of new types of work organization such as call centres, central to which is the focus on women as those most likely to possess the skills necessary for work of this type.

One of the concepts developed in Hochschild's work is the concept of the development of 'care-chains' which have emerged with the globalization of domestic labour. Migrant women from the Philippines, Indonesia, Thailand, Burma and Sri Lanka are employed with few rights and in difficult situations. Women frequently see their children just once a year and their own children are living with relatives or other employed helpers. Their relationships with their children are often very difficult and migrant domestic workers send happy photographs of themselves and their fellow workers to conceal the difficulties and abuse they frequently suffer. Hochschild (2003b) describes the situation of Vicky Diaz, a college-educated Filipina who is currently employed in Los Angeles earning US$400 a week, working as a nanny in a wealthy American family. She pays a live-in worker in the Philippines 40 dollars a week to look after her family of five. In the last nine years she has only spent three months with her family and is actively trying to move them to the US.

Salazar Parreñas (2001b: 371) shows how the emotional strains of transnational mothering include feelings of anxiety, helplessness, loss, guilt, and the burden of loneliness. She notes that the domestic migrant women justify their decisions to leave their children behind in the Philippines by highlighting the material gains of the family. They struggle to maintain a semblance of family life by rationalizing distance. She shows that 'A few women explicitly deny the emotional strains imposed by separation on their children, most women admit to the emotional difficulties that they themselves feel.' Salazar Parreñas notes that:

> On average, they visit their children every four years for a period of two months. They attribute the infrequency of their return to the high cost of airfare and to the fact that they cannot afford to take time off work. In addition, the fear of losing their jobs prevents them from visiting their families for an extended period of time. As they are limited to short visits to the Philippines, travelling is seen as an excessive expense of funds that could otherwise be used on meeting the costs of reproducing the family.

In fact, very few countries in the world allow migrant Filipina domestic workers or other migrant workers family reunification. They include Canada, the US, and Italy. However, many structural factors deter migrant Filipina domestic workers in these countries from sponsoring the migration of their children. For instance, the occupational demands of domestic work make it difficult for them to raise their children in these host countries. In Italy, low wages force most day workers to work long hours. In the United States, most are live-in domestic workers. As such, their work arrangement limits the time they can devote to the care of their own families.

Hondagneu-Sotelo and Avila (1997) in discussing the position of live-in and live-out workers in Los Angeles point out that live-in jobs are the least compatible with conventional mothering responsibilities. Employers who hire live-in workers do so because they generally want employees for jobs that may require round-the-clock service. They cite an owner of a domestic employment agency:

> They [employers] want a live-in to have somebody at their beck and call. They want the hours that are most difficult for them covered, which is like six thirty in the morning 'till eight when the kids go to school, and four to seven when the kids are home, and its homework, bath and dinner.
>
> (ibid.: 555)

They note that live-in workers work on average 64 hours per week. The best live-in worker, from an employer's perspective, is one without daily family obligations of her own:

> The workweek may consist of six very long workdays. These may span from dawn to midnight and include overnight responsibilities with sleepless or sick children, making it virtually impossible for live-in workers to sustain daily contact with their own families. Although some employers do allow for their employees' children to live in as well (Romeros 1996), this is rare . . . In fact, minimal family and mothering obligations are an informal job placement criterion for live-in workers. Many of the agencies specializing in the placement of live-in nanny-housekeepers will not even refer a woman who has children in Los Angeles to interviews for live-in jobs.
>
> (ibid.)

Hondagneu-Sotelo and Avila also note that the less than minimum pay and the long hours for live-in workers make it very difficult for these workers to have their children in the United States. Some live-in workers who have children in the same city as their place of employment hire their own nanny-housekeeper, often a younger female relative to care for the children. They note that most transnational mothers come to the US with the intention to stay for a finite period of time, until they can support their family financially.

Conclusion

Globalization has led to a demand for high-level professional workers, with more women finding themselves in corporate professional jobs. Single professionals and two career households prefer cosmopolitan living and, as Sassen (2003) notes, this results in an expansion of high-income residential areas in global cities and a return to family life, albeit on a different basis. These include the servicing of the emotional labour needs of high-end professionals in global cities in the Asia-Pacific, Europe, the US and the Middle East. Globalization and global cities have thus become places where large numbers of low-paid women and immigrants are incorporated into strategic economic sectors. Yet those countries do not acknowledge the added value of such a workforce (see Chapter 6). The 'commercialization of intimate life' in global economies is one way in which women executives attempt to address emotional labour demands. The more recent economic downturn globally is likely to have an impact on global cities and labour force participation. The impact on professional women and on emotional labour remains to be seen.

6 Servicing high-end professional populations

Female migrant labour as a transnational community

Ann Brooks

Introduction

Transnational labour migration is a feature of globalization which has become increasingly 'feminized' (see Chapter 3) with Hong Kong, Malaysia, Singapore, as well as Canada, the US and the Middle East being key destinations for female migrant domestic labour. This chapter examines transnational female migrant labour servicing the emotional labour needs of high-end professionals, both ex-patriots, and local communities in global cities in Asia, the US, Europe and the Middle East. The conceptualization of female migrant domestic labour as a trans-national community is an important one and, as Salazar Parreñas (2001b) notes, it is the result of simultaneously a structural and cultural process, and is in response to the kinds of pressures the female migrants are faced with in the country where they work, as well as a response to the country and families they have left behind. This chapter examines a number of issues around female migrant labour as a trans-national community including: human rights issues, the emotional labour or par-enting implications of transnational female migrants, and examines what impact it is having on female domestic migrants' identity and their relationship with their children and families in their country of origin.

The entry of emotional labour debates into the considerations of work and organizations has occurred alongside other significant developments concerning the growth in the service economy and the 'feminization' of local labour markets (see Chapter 3). This has led to a greater need to focus on the eliciting of desired emotions in the provision of service and has placed emotion work and emotional labour at the forefront of analysis. It has also led to a global explosion in the trans-migration of female domestic labour to meet the emotional demands of profes-sional women and families in a number of countries.

In addition, transnational labour markets are also changing, as Salazar Parreñas (2001b: 368) notes:

> In newly industrialized countries such as Taiwan and Malaysia, globaliza-tion and the rise of manufacturing production have also generated a demand for low-wage service migrant workers. Production activities in these econo-mies have subsumed the traditional proletariat female work-force who would

otherwise perform low-wage service jobs, such as domestic work. This shift in labour market concentration has generated a need for the lower wage labour of women from neighbouring countries in Asia, to fill the demand for service employment.

Globalization and the servicing of emotional labour

One of the ways in which parents have sought to combine a career with family life in some countries has been through the growth of a female migrant domestic labour market. In her book *Domestica,* Pierre Hondagneu-Sotelo (2001) described a 'new world domestic order' in which the increasing domestic and childcare needs in affluent nations are filled by low-paid immigrants from developing countries. One of the largest sources of independent female labour migrants in the world, the Philippines has seen, as a result, the formation of a growing number of female-headed transnational families. These families are households with core members living in at least two nation-states and in which the mother works as domestic labourer in another country while some or all of her dependants reside in the Philippines.

Globalization has led to a significant movement in migrant labour to accommodate the emotional labour demands of what Salazar Parreñas (2001b) has called the high-end 'servants of globalization'. They consist of highly skilled, well-heeled, First World professionals who are either expatriate migrants in countries such as the Middle East and parts of Asia or part of a growing number of local professional women and dual career families in Asia, the US and Europe. These 'high-end' professionals face a range of pressures from increased competition, workplace and time pressures. The rise in the international 'maid trade' is a significant aspect of the 'commercialization of intimate life' (Hochschild 2003a, 2003b). These flows of migrant labour, particularly female migrant labour, to work as domestic servants have benefited professional and middle-class women and families in a number of countries. Working-class, minority and migrant women are preferred labour for certain kinds of jobs, particularly childcare and domestic labour.

The feminization of labour migration is particularly pronounced in the Philippines, Indonesia and Sri Lanka. In these countries, national estimates indicate that women comprise 60–75 per cent of legal migrants, a significant proportion of whom are employed as domestic workers in the Middle East, Singapore, Malaysia and Hong Kong. For labour-sending countries such as Indonesia, the Philippines, Sri Lanka, India, and Thailand, the 'export' of labour has become an increasingly important strategy to address unemployment, generate foreign exchange and foster economic growth. The question is, to what extent do these widely dispersed groups have an incipient desire to appeal to a conception of a transnational community, both to act to represent a wide diversity of interests and to advocate on behalf of female domestic migrants?

Many Asian women migrants are domestic workers and are particularly at risk of workplace abuse and exploitation because of the isolated nature of their work and lack of legal protection. Labour laws around the world usually exclude domestic work from regulation. Salazar Parreñas (2001b) refers to the 'partial citizenship' of low-wage migrant workers who experience 'stunted integration . . . in receiving nation-states', which we can see clearly in these cases where women domestic workers are denied basic civic and reproductive rights. She also notes that embedded in this 'international reproduction of labour' (Salazar Parreñas 2000) are structural inequalities in access to care among women and families that are produced and reproduced through social policy and everyday practice.

For example, the case of migrant workers in Singapore highlights some of these issues. The combination of Singaporean women's increasing labour force participation, a private sector that has failed to innovate 'family-friendly' working conditions, and few feasible child care options has led to a strong demand for foreign domestic workers. Singapore introduced the Foreign Maid Scheme in 1978. This programme opened the door for women from the Philippines, Indonesia, Thailand, Burma, Sri Lanka, India and Bangladesh to enter Singapore as 'live-in' domestic workers. The migrant domestic labour force grew from 5,000 in 1978 to the current level of 190,000 (this figure is cited in Devasahayam 2010).

In 2005, 150,000 female migrant domestic workers worked in Singapore, from Indonesia, the Philippines and Sri Lanka. One in every six households employs a domestic worker known as 'helpers' or 'maids'. This cuts across social classes and even the poorest households have a maid. The treatment of women domestic workers has frequently led to international criticism, with significant maid abuse and lack of basic human rights. Immigration policies prohibit the marriage of foreign domestic workers to Singapore citizens. Women domestic workers are also obliged to undergo medical examination every six months, including pregnancy and HIV tests. If they are found to be pregnant, they face dismissal and deportation. Singapore is not alone in its policies, Salazar Parreñas (2001b) states that various countries limit the term of the settlement to temporary labour contracts and deny entry to their spouses and children. As a result, migrant Filipina domestic workers with children are forced to mother from a distance. As Salazar Parreñas (ibid.: 369) states:

> The liberal states of the United States and Italy are not exempt from the trend of 'renationalization'. In the United States, for example, lawmakers are entertaining the promotion of temporary labour migration and the elimination of certain preference categories for family reunification, including the preference categories for adult children and parents of U.S. citizens and permanent residents – the trend being to continue the labor provided by migrants but to discontinue support for their reproduction. In Italy, the 'guest worker' status of migrant Filipinos coupled with their restricted options in the labor market encourages the maintenance of transnational households.

Parenting issues within the community of female migrant labour

The parenting and emotional labour issues confronting professional women in the Asia-Pacific and the US more generally are clearly different from those of transnational female domestic migrant workers, however, the emotional labour issues this latter group experiences are as problematic as those of professional women. A primary worry among transnational mothers, as noted by Hondagneu-Sotelo and Avila (1997), is that their children are being neglected or abused in their absence. They are uncertain as to whether their children are receiving the full financial support they send home. They also note that transnational female domestic migrants see caregiving as a defining feature of the mothering experience, and while they rationalize their distance from their own children in terms of improvements in lifestyle and access to education, they also worry about some of the negative effects on their children. Hondagneu-Sotelo and Avila (ibid.: 563) outline the views of one female migrant domestic worker from El Salvador:

> Gladys who had four of her five children in El Salvador acknowledged that her US dollar went further in El Salvador. Although she missed seeing those four children grow up, she felt that in some ways, she had spared them the indignities to which she had exposed her youngest daughter, whom she brought to the United States at age 4 . . . her live-in employer had initially quarantined her daughter, insisting on seeing vaccination papers before allowing the girl to play with the employer's children. 'I had to battle, really struggle' she recalled, 'just to get enough food for her (to eat).'

The transnational community of female migrant domestic workers attempts to combine caregiving with breadwinning. While the work they do may require them to establish long periods of time apart from their children, they make huge efforts to sustain family connections through letters, phone calls and money sent home. They make efforts to travel home to visit their children. They maintain their mothering responsibilities across national boundaries.

The emotional needs of transnational female domestic migrants are sometimes evidenced in the development of strong ties of affection with the children they care for. These nannies and domestic workers spend large amounts of time alone with the children. Carolina, a Guatemalan woman with four children between the ages of 10–14 in her home country, said that she tried to treat the children of her employer with the same affection she treated her own.

Another feature of many of the transnational female domestic migrants is that they are highly critical in private of what they perceive as the employers' neglectful parenting and mothering. They blame the biological mothers for substandard parenting. This case of Carolina is recalled by Hondagneu-Sotelo and Avila (1997: 565): 'Carolina recalled advising the mother . . . that the girl [her daughter] needed to receive more affection from her mother, whom she perceived as self-absorbed with physical fitness regimes.' Carolina also commented that when she advised her current employer to spend more than 15 minutes a day with the baby, the employer had been reduced to tears. The justification for transnational migration on the part of female domestic workers is not extended by them to their employers.

There is an interesting comparison between transnational female migrants working in the US and those working in Asia. While the profiles of the female migrants are similar, it is unlikely that the domestic workers in Asia would feel able to make the same kind of comment to their employers as those working in the US do. As Hondagneu-Sotelo and Avila (ibid.: 566) note:

> The Latina nannies appear to endorse motherhood as a full-time vocation in contexts of sufficient financial resources, but in contexts of financial hardship such as their own, they advocate more elastic definitions of motherhood, including forms that may include long spatial and temporal separations of mother and children.

Human rights issues and female migrant labour

The transnational community of female migrant domestic labour share a range of abuses of human rights, regardless of which country they find themselves in. They have few or no human rights, which range from minor restrictions to major human rights issues. Abuses include long working hours, number of days off, restrictions on freedom of movement and association, lack of pay, and physical and sexual abuse. Migrant domestic workers have little access to the justice system due to the restrictions on their movement, lack of information about their rights, and language barriers.

Migrant domestic workers are often isolated from other employees, friends or family. Many cannot communicate in the language of the host country, are undocumented, or lack adequate contracts. Under the sponsorship system in countries of the Gulf Cooperation Council (GCC), for example, employers hold the passports and all other documents until the date of departure, rendering the domestic worker completely dependent. In addition, in some Arab and Asian countries, domestic workers are indebted to labour agencies for the costs of recruitment, travel and processing fees. These agencies often withhold payment for several months following arrival. If domestic workers break their contract even in cases of abuse, they are often forced to forfeit their paycheque and, for those who can afford it, pay their own airfare home. Most domestic workers who suffer severe human rights violations have to remain with their employers for fear of deportation or loss of legal status. They fear losing the jobs that sustain their families at home and worry that employers and recruitment agents will 'blacklist' them for future employment.

The most extreme forms of exploitation and abuse have resulted in severe injury and even death. The International Labour Organization maintains that many migrant workers from Sri Lanka, the Philippines and Indonesia have died in unclear circumstances. In Singapore, between 1999 and 2005, an estimated 147 domestic workers died, most by falling out of buildings or committing suicide. In 2004, the Asia Pacific Forum on Women, Law and Development (APWLD) reported on cases of violent assaults and deaths of domestic workers in Lebanon, Kuwait, Malaysia and Saudi Arabia. In the latter case 19,000 domestic workers fled from their employers in 2000. In 2005, an NGO in Israel testified in the case of a female migrant domestic labourer who was physically assaulted when she tried to take a day off and threatened with further violence when she demanded full pay for her work. There are also other examples, for instance, in 2005, the Global Rights and the American Civil Liberties Union reported abuses involving UN diplomats and staff. Abusive employers are rarely prosecuted and convicted, although in Hong Kong and Singapore several cases of severe ill-treatment have appeared in court.

In addition to specific cases of violence and abuse against migrant domestic workers, they also face an increased risk of HIV infection and are vulnerable to violations to their reproductive rights. For example, in Sri Lanka where migrants often undergo testing, almost half of all reported HIV cases occurred among domestic workers who had returned from the Middle East. In a 2002 survey of domestic workers in Hong Kong, those surveyed reported various sexual and reproductive health problems that revealed limited access to health information and services, as well as the stigma attached to seeking them. In 2003, the Saudi Arabian Ministry of Health prohibited pregnant domestic workers from accessing health services unless accompanied by the father. This puts women whose husbands are abroad, or those who have become pregnant as a result of rape, in a very difficult situation.

The maltreatment of women domestic workers has raised international criticism. This was the case in the relations between Singapore and its neighbours. A major political dispute erupted between the Philippines and Singapore when a Filipina domestic worker, Flor Contemplacion, was sentenced to death and executed for murdering another Filipina domestic worker and a child in 1995. The response from the Philippines was to suspend its workers from working in Singapore. In recent years, Indonesian groups have protested at the deaths of Indonesian workers convicted of crimes. They have called for greater investigation into abuses and working conditions that have contributed to deaths and crimes. In September 2005, two Indonesian domestic workers, facing death sentences for killing a Singaporean employer, received a life sentence and a ten-year prison term instead of being sentenced to death. They were convicted of 'culpable homicide' in recognition of employment abuses they had suffered. More recently, Indonesia has refused to send female migrant workers to Malaysia due to ill-treatment of their nationals.

Different governments have responded to the criticisms of the treatment of female domestic migrants and have attempted to improve the human rights and treatment of workers. The Hong Kong labour laws guarantee a minimum wage, maternity leave, a weekly day off, public holidays and paid vacation time. The governments of Malaysia and the Philippines have negotiated a standard contract for Filipina domestic workers covering similar protections. In Singapore, the legal age for domestic workers has been raised to 23, there are increased prosecutions for abusive employers, an obligatory orientation programme for domestic workers and employers, and a telephone information service that instructs workers in their rights to change employers.

In 2003, Bahrain launched a national plan to support abused foreign workers that also provides a telephone hotline and shelters. The embassies of Indonesia, the Philippines and Sri Lanka all maintain mechanisms for fielding and addressing labour complaints, including offering assistance to secure legal advice and medical care. Hong Kong and Italy allow women migrant domestic workers to organize into migrant unions. The first Asian Migrant Workers Summit was held in Hong Kong in 2007, this was held in Hong Kong City University.

The issue of the rights and abuses of female migrant domestic workers, particularly in Southeast Asia, is part of a wider discussion on rights and citizenship. Ong (2006) in her analysis of neo-liberalism, citizenship and rights, maintains that market skills and conceptions of human worth are strategic determinants of rights and citizenship. As Ong (ibid.: 16) shows:

> In global circuits, educated and self-propulsive individuals claim citizenship-like entitlements and benefits, even at the expense of the territorialized citizens. Expatriate talents constitute a form of moveable entitlement without formal citizenship . . . Citizens who are deemed too complacent or lacking in neoliberal potential may be treated as less-worthy subjects. Low-skill citizens and migrants become exceptions to neoliberal mechanisms and are constructed as excludable populations in transit, shunted in and out of zones of growth.

One dimension of the intersection of neo-liberalism with both rights and citizenship can be seen in the way in which economic globalization has resulted in patterns of labour-based transmigration with large numbers of workers excluded from rights of citizenship and other rights. As Ong (ibid.: 23) shows:

> Despite legal citizenship in some countries, millions of migrant workers, refugees and trafficked peoples who have the most minimal hold on survival have become more imperiled and elusive. It is clear that legal citizenship is merely one form of human protection. Marginalised peoples are excluded from an environment of rights because they are all, often, hidden from view, or live in 'failed states' or as displaced peoples they are effectively stripped of rights once on the move.

Ong's argument is that traditional models of citizenship are being 'disarticulated' as entitlements regarding political membership and national territory are given to those with clearly marketable skills that are highly valued by society. These rights are subsequently denied to those who are judged to lack such capacity.

This is particularly interesting in the context of Singapore where a city-state with a seriously declining population, and one which is now extending its citizenship rights to large numbers of foreign migrants, maintains tight policies of exclusion when it comes to the large contingent of female migrant domestic workers, who serve to maintain an entire dimension of professional women in the labour force in Singapore and provide a servicing dimension to the Singapore economy, and who gain no recognition, even from those who directly benefit from it. It is perhaps surprising that the professionals who act reflectively as regards their own patterns of intimacy are so prepared to remain oblivious to the abuses of the rights of intimacy and access to citizenship for the very domestic workers who support them.

'Biopolitical otherness'[1]

Ong (2006: 199) maintains that ethnicity is an important factor in asserting an identity against 'the biopolitical other':

> This racialist opposition is reinforced by moral schemes that are sceptical about the attachability of mobile, alien women detached from their own moral communities. The biopolitical concerns of wealthier nations to secure middle-class entitlements depend on the availability of foreign others, creating an environment of class privilege and bias that tolerates slave-like conditions for poor female migrants.

The female domestic migrant community is not valued for their contribution, but, on the contrary, is considered both as undesirable aliens as well as a threat to the security of the nation, by threatening ethnic elitism and undermining the social fabric of society because of their sexuality. A hierarchy of ethnicity also holds when it comes to foreign domestic labour: Filipina workers are well educated with high-level English skills and are seen as more prestigious and are more expensive to employ. Despite this, in Hong Kong they are constructed as social inferiors. However, the large number of Filipinas working in Hong Kong and the recognition by this group of their contribution and worth, encourage them to assert their identity in public spaces on Sunday and they hold street festivals, and parades to establish their presence in the society (Constable 1997).

In Singapore, 'foreign maids' are considered by the local community to be a 'necessary evil' and their weekend locations are seen as 'no go areas' by the local middle classes: 'So despite the gloss of Westernized cultural skills, Filipina maids operate as a ubiquitous, contrastive, racial or alien other to the dominant ethnic Chinese population' (Ong 2006: 203). Foreign maids from other ethnic backgrounds and countries in the region, e.g. Indonesia, India, Sri Lanka, and Thailand, are treated as both ethnic and social inferiors. Particularly vitriolic treatment and attitudes are directed towards Indonesians. They are seen as 'illegal' migrants regardless of their contractual position. They are the subject of significant abuse and this is highlighted in an article in *The Straits Times*, of 20 June 2009, entitled 'Jakarta stops sending maids to Malaysia from today',[2] where the Indonesian government responded to the outrage over the abuse of one of its nationals working as a 'domestic helper' in Malaysia. Ong maintains that Indonesian workers are always assessed in terms of the likelihood of being illegal and a threat to the community. Indonesia has come to see itself as a 'coolie nation', serving its richer neighbours. There is little doubt that the lack of skills and competence associated with Indonesians reinforces the racism which positions them as socially inferior. As Ong (ibid.: 203) observes:

> The scramble to become 'global cities' has led to the reinforcement of laws against public expressions of racism in Hong Kong, Singapore and Kuala Lumpur, but these rules do not apply when it comes to the treatment of foreign migrants who perform a variety of 'low-skill' or 'un-skilled jobs'

avoided by local citizens. But the daily intimate association with these 'backward' racial others threatens to subvert the self-image of well-heeled Asians, who themselves have so recently sloughed off menial labour and paddy fields. There is a suppressed fear that the increasing presence of poor migrants will blur the ethno-racial distinction of the nation, which in post-colonial Asia is based on ideological constructions of race, kinship, language, religion and culture.

The way in which Filipino and Indonesian maids are supported by their nation-state also has implications. Filipino maids are presented as 'labor aristocracy' (ibid.) supported by the Philippine government and NGOs who value these women for their 'export value' and who represent these women as well-educated, linguistically skilled, professional workers, worthy of respect. By contrast, Indonesian authorities and NGOs have not supported Indonesian female migrants in the same way. However, recent action by Indonesia taken against Malaysia for abuses of Indonesian migrants signals a change in attitude by Indonesian authorities (see note 2).

Ong maintains that 'technologies of incarceration','securitization', and 'sterility' are all employed against female domestic migrant labour. Foreign maids employed in Singapore, Malaysia and Hong Kong are subject to a largely 'incarcerated' existence in houses that employ them. In these countries they can apply for the renewal of contract but not for citizenship.

In Singapore, for example, work permits confine domestic workers solely to 'duties of a domestic nature' within a single employer's household. The implication of this is that the foreign maid cannot take up any part-time employment elsewhere even on her day(s) off. Foreign maids will be fined and deported if found to be breaching this agreement although many do have additional cleaning and other work which they organize illegally and privately. In Hong Kong, foreign maids get special work visas that ensure minimum wages and days off. In Singapore and Malaysia, there are rules regulating the work conditions of female migrant domestic labour and it is left to the 'free market' to determine both wages and conditions. As Ong (ibid.: 202) states:

> The unregulated nature of domestic employment is based on a logic of incarceration. The employer contracts every aspect of a foreign maid's life. It is common practice in Singapore and Malaysia for the employer to hold the maid's passport and work papers, on the pretext of preventing her from running away, but in effect confining her within the household. The employer thus gains a de facto ownership over the foreign domestic, who is thus made vulnerable to exploitation of her labour and sexuality.

The aftermath of the Asian financial crisis (1997–98) resulted in 900,000 migrant workers, the majority of whom were female, being expelled from their positions. In addition, incidents of torture and murder of maids also increased. Ong (ibid.: 206) maintains that the tensions between the perception of foreign maids as 'racially and socially contaminating' and their involvement in intimate social relationships 'engender complex mechanisms of internal exclusion'. She argues that there are three factors which she sees as inherent within the ethnic and racial topography of the countries in the Southeast Asian region, which result in 'biopolitical othering' and abuse of foreign maids.

The first factor Ong identifies is characteristic of ethnic Chinese populations whether diasporic or not, which is the practice of 'servitude'. Ong (ibid.: 206) outlines the relationship of servitude:

> First, among ethnic Chinese populations, there is a historic practice of servi-tude that constructs the unattached mobile woman as an unprotected category. Many in Southeast Asia are familiar with the *mui-jai* (Cantonese) or bonded maidservant who faithfully served a single family throughout her life. In the early twentieth century, *mui-jai* were young unattached girls who could be bought and sold as a form of dowry for concubinage, prostitution or slavery. The *mui-jai* was therefore an essential outsider, marked by her kinless state and thus assigned a slave status. A more pejorative term was *yong-yan*, an individual for the personal use of the owner. The *mui-jai* could only overcome her social condition by becoming attached through kinship to the employer's family. The enslavement of poor, unattached young women was a pervasive practice throughout the British colonies of Southeast Asia. In 1921, the new professional class in Hong Kong led the fight against the *mui-jai*, in the name of support for female liberation.

It is the particular set of ethnic, racial relations and the role of the foreign maid which make her susceptible to being considered a *mui-jai* or bonded maidservant. Foreign maids are frequently not ethnic Chinese, therefore they can never be seen as kin. As Ong (ibid.: 207) states:'The Filipina or Indonesian maid is an intoler-able alien to the moral economy of many Chinese families.'

Second, Ong maintains that the short-term contract of the foreign maid frus-trates the employer as after she has been 'trained' into domestic chores, which meet the needs of the middle-class Chinese family, she leaves (see Chin 1998). In addition, she is seen to waste family resources, even the limited resources expended on most maids.

Third, there is the sexual dimension of having a foreign maid who is young, exotic, can frequently speak much better English than the average Chinese wife and thus stirs jealousy and anxiety. The foreign maid is seen as someone who 'entraps' the male employer and brings rape as an abuse upon herself. It is not sur-prising, given these factors, that it is the female employer who is most likely to see the foreign maid as an economic and sexual threat and it is the wife/employer who is most likely to abuse the foreign maid. Ong (2006: 208) notes that this pattern of behaviour is in no way restricted to middle-class Chinese families:

> In Malaysia, even the moral economies of Malay Muslims and their Indonesian maids, while having in common Islam, race and similar *kampong* (village) derived cultures, do not always guarantee good treatment for the

latter. Domestic workers from Indonesia are viewed as 'social pariahs' undeserving of public sympathy.

Not only are female migrant domestic labourers the subject of incarceration, securitization and abuse, they are also subjected to 'technologies of sterility'. This is related to limiting the foreign maid's capacity for sexuality and intimacy. During the period of the contract, the foreign maid is not permitted to have sex or to marry a local citizen. In relation to the last point, and to ensure the foreign maid cannot claim citizenship, she is tested every six months for HIV and pregnancy. If the foreign maid is found to be pregnant, it results in the immediate termination of the contract and her expulsion from the country. All aspects of health care are left to the employer. The foreign maid is thus devoid of her biological rights and 'cannot express corporeal desires' (ibid.: 208). She is thus denied her reproductive rights.

Conclusion

Transnational female migrant labour can be framed as a transnational community not just in spatial and geographical terms by being located across national boundaries, but also by being constructed simultaneously as a set of structural and cultural processes which give these migrants a clear identity. These include the servicing of the emotional labour needs of high-end professionals in global cities in the Asia-Pacific, Europe, the US and the Middle East. Their framing as a transnational community is in response to the kinds of pressures they are faced with in the country they migrate to work, as well as a response to the countries and families they have left behind in their country of origin. Their identity is constructed by the pressures of providing a better life for their families and thus is motivated by financial imperatives as well as by the priorities of maintaining close bonds with their family of origin. Their identity is also framed by the kinds of human rights issues which characterize their daily lives, which include both small and major violations of their rights. It also includes their relationships with both the families they have left behind and the families they care for. There has been an increasing realization in different countries of the need to address the rights of this transnational community and to recognize their significant contribution to the global economy.

Notes

1 I am grateful to Aiwha Ong (2006) for the use of the concept 'Biopolitical otherness'.
2 The article from Agence France Presse, appearing in *The Straits Times* (Singapore), outlines the case of a domestic helper who was brutally treated by her employers in Malaysia. The Indonesian government has as a result suspended the sending of foreign maids to Malaysia until a new agreement is reached on the treatment of foreign workers. *The Straits Times* article reports:

> Just last week, a 43 year old Malaysian woman was charged with causing grievous bodily harm to an Indonesian domestic helper by allegedly beating her with a cane and dowsing her with boiling water. Pictures of Ms Siti Hajar with horrific scars all

over her body were splashed across newspapers. The 33 year old from East Java was reportedly tortured by her Malaysian female employer for three years . . . Ms Siti Hajar finally escaped from her employer's condominium apartment late one night . . . She hid in a drain until sunrise when she persuaded a taxi driver to take her to the Indonesian Embassy.

7 Men, masculinities and emotional labour

Ann Brooks

Introduction

Increasing emphasis is being given to the relationship between men, masculinity(ies) and emotional labour. A number of factors or trends have led to this increased emphasis including: demographic factors, such as the increase in the divorce rate and the number of single parent families headed by women; the changing nature of work and organizations which requires a more internationally mobile workforce and which blurs the work–life balance; the relationship between social class and emotional capital; the growth in opportunities for women executives; the increased availability and mobility of a domestic service industry providing emotional and domestic labour; the retention of a gendered hierarchical model of emotional labour in career-oriented couples; on-going gender discrimination in organizational structures; men in female-dominated occupations; and the commercialization of emotional labour globally. The first section of the chapter reviews the literature in the field based on these social trends. The second section of the chapter considers the implications for the relationship between men, masculinities and emotional labour in organizational and domestic domains. Conclusions are drawn in considering the implications of the current trends for a democratization of emotional labour in work and domestic contexts.

Demographic factors, divorce and emotional labour

Demographic factors have highlighted the issue of emotional labour as regards parenting responsibilities. Hochschild (2003a) notes that in most of the advanced industrial world the divorce rate has risen, and with it the number of single parent families. She notes that in America, the divorce rate has increased to 50 per cent and that one-fifth of the households are headed by single mothers. She also notes that most of these single mothers get little financial help from their ex-husbands and most work full-time outside the home.

The pattern of single parent families is frequently not a temporary one and Hochschild (ibid.: 215) also notes that a third of single mothers never remarry and of the two-thirds who do remarry, over half divorce again. She comments that:

In 2000, 18 percent of children under age eighteen were living with single mothers and 4 percent with single fathers. Since the remarriage rate for women is lower than that for men (because men tend to marry younger women), and since divorced women are far more likely to gain custody of children, most single parents are women. Divorced men provide much less care for their children, than married men, and divorced women much more.

In addition to the increasing numbers of single parent families headed by women, the emotional bonds between fathers and children also becomes more distant with divorce. Hochschild (ibid.: 216) notes that fathers are not only physically absent after divorce but that they also have reduced contact with their children and give them less money. Citing a national survey in the US, she found that:

> Three years after divorce, half of American divorced fathers had not visited their children during the previous year and thus did not perform the basic form of care. After one year, half of divorced fathers were providing no child support at all, and most of the other half paid irregularly or less than court designated payments.

There is little or no evidence of a class differential in the kind of support provided and Hochschild notes that wealthy divorced fathers were just as unlikely to be negligent as poor ones. As Hochschild observes: 'Certain demographic shifts and family decline have shifted the population in need of care, radically reduced social support on the home front, and moved a good deal of the burden of care from men to women' (ibid.: 216).

In addition to the demographic trends outlined above, there has also been an increase in the number of single parents who are unmarried women. There has been an increase in the proportion of all births throughout the developed world (with the exception of Japan). Hochschild (ibid.: 216) notes that the percentage has increased from 23 per cent in 1986 to 33 per cent in 2000. The highest rates are found in the US, Denmark, Sweden, France and the UK. The pattern as outlined by Hochschild is for single mothers to cohabit with the fathers of their children but the rate of break-up is higher for cohabitating than for married couples. So the burden of emotional labour falls more heavily on single mothers.

Overall the pattern of emotional labour in domestic domains emerging from changing demographic patterns shows a gendered division of care work, regardless of the fact that men do contribute to emotional labour in the home. As Coltrane and Galt (2000: 30) observe: 'Mothers are still more likely than fathers to take time off from their jobs to provide continuous childcare, spending significantly more time than fathers, feeding, dressing, cleaning and watching young children.'

Emotional capital

The debate around emotional labour has traditionally not been grounded within a theoretical framework nor has it involved an analysis of class. More recently,

Reay (2004) has framed emotional labour within a broader analysis of Bourdieu's understanding of cultural capital. While Bourdieu does not refer explicitly to emotional capital, he does see the centrality of the family within cultural capital, and recognizes the contribution of women, and specifically the mother in this regard. In *Masculine Domination* (2001: 77), Bourdieu observes that: 'Women fulfil a cathartic, quasi-therapeutic function in regulating men's emotional lives, calming their anger, helping them accept the injustices and difficulties of life.' Reay also notes that women engage in emotional labour more than men and act to reduce anxiety and distress. However, Lovell (2000) has noted the lack of value given to 'emotional capital' due to its association with the domestic/familial sphere, although labour market capital accumulation strategies do credit women as subjects with strategies of their own. Lovell defines this in terms of symbolic, social and cultural capital and its reproduction across generations. Reay notes that working-class women lack reserves of capital which make it difficult to transmit emotional capital. She also notes that emotional well-being is more easily achieved in circumstances of privilege.

Links between emotional capital and social class is a close one and is specifically related to the class context of mothers. Hays (1996), in the *Cultural Contradictions of Motherhood*, interviewed middle-class working women and stay-at-home mothers and working-class stay-at-home mothers and concludes that the ideology of intensive mothering is a quintessentially urban middle-class and upper middle-class white syndrome. She argues that single mothers and those from the lower income strata of society are unlikely to subscribe to such an intense ideology because they lack economic and cultural capital. Thus, the claims made by Hochschild (2003a) that the increase in demographic patterns for the numbers of single mothers can be equated with an increase in emotional labour for women need to be qualified by an analysis of class.

Bourdieu (2000) acknowledged the inseparability of gender and class. However, he failed to pay attention to the relationship between gender and capital. Bourdieu did not see gender as a form of capital and it has been left to subsequent theorists (Lovell 2000; McCall 1992; Reay 2004; Skeggs 2004) to further develop the relationship. Lovell (2000: 21), for example, argues that Bourdieu saw women as capital-bearing 'objects' rather than 'subjects'. The implication of this is that Bourdieu saw women as playing a significant part in the accumulation of capital for men but did not see women as having the potential for capital accumulation strategies of their own. Hence, as has been noted by Lovell (2000: 22) and McNay (2000:142), women are 'repositories' of capital.

The relationship between gender and class in understanding the potential for the concept of capital in relation to emotional capital has been developed by a number of theorists (Illouz 1997; Lovell 2000; Reay 2004; Skeggs 1997). Reay and Illouz specifically address the relationship between emotional capital, gender and class. Both theorists maintain that Bourdieu has overlooked the concept of emotional capital. Reay understands emotional capital in her work as about 'investment in others rather than self' (Reay 2004: 71). Reay, as noted, sees emotional capital as both gendered and classed. Working-class women, Reay maintains, are distracted from emotional capital by more pressing concerns such as poverty. She maintains that conditions of poverty are not those conducive to providing emotional capital.

Huppatz (2009) examines a further development of the concept of capital, drawing on Bourdieu to examine two forms of gendered capital: feminine and female capital in the context of paid caring work. Huppatz maintains that feminine capital can be seen to operate in this field as both symbolic capital and subsequently economic capital. However, she notes that feminine and female capital are tactical rather than strategic as they do not carry institutional backing (ibid.: 60). Thus, she maintains, their use-value is limited.

Emotional labour and executive men

In her early work on the relationship between emotional labour and corporate life, Hochschild's (1997: 59) study of *Amerco* highlights the views of corporate men on the issue of emotional labour. As one executive commented referring to his relationship with his wife:

> We made a bargain. If I was going to be as successful as we both wanted, I was going to have to spend tremendous amounts of time at work. Her end of the bargain was that she wouldn't go out to work. So I was able to take the good stuff and she did the hard work – car pools, dinner, gymnastic lessons.

In their study of stockbrokers, Blair-Loy and Jacobs (2003) found a very traditional marriage pattern among brokers. Most of the male stockbrokers are the major breadwinners and 66 per cent have wives who are homemakers or who hold part-time jobs. They note that among the married fathers, 75 per cent are homemakers or employed part-time. Emotional labour obligations are frequently stressful for the executive men, as one male executive commented:

> I leave the house at 6.30 every morning, maybe earlier. So I don't see my family as much as I'd like to. But I think that, you know you have to pay those dues to go forward. And it's worked out well. So you know . . . I mean, the bottom line is somebody's got to pay the bills in life. I would love to sit home with my wife and child but that's not real, that's not gonna happen.
>
> (ibid.: 240)

The emotional labour obligations of the family on top of the stressful work environment resulted in a strong desire for personal space among some executives. Some executive men found the time with family more stressful than being at work. One executive describes what he calls 'sanity time' which includes playing golf, working out at the gym and seeing friends:

> I don't want to spend too much time away from home, but I don't want to spend too much time at home . . . I work hard . . . But then I also have to take

care of myself, so I exercise. So I don't come home [right after work] and feel like I'm going straight from work to home and I'm taking care of a new baby and I didn't have time for me. And I don't want to feel resentful for that.

(ibid.)

While this situation seems very reasonable, Blair-Loy and Jacobs (ibid.: 239) found some resentment from the wives interviewed who wished their broker husbands would spend more time with families and less time on 'creative personal space'. Cindy Smooth, a wife of one of the executives, admitted that her husband spent a lot of time on the golf course and not much time with their son: 'He golfs a lot . . . I would be happier if he takes care of our son on weekends once or twice a month.'

The higher level of reflexivity shown by executive men in relation to an understanding of their own social and personal needs in a work context is not extended to sharing the emotional labour obligations within the family. There is little evidence of any democratization of relationships from the examples drawn on here.

Professional men clearly often find home life more stressful than worklife. A study coming out of Australia found that balancing demands of home and work was more stressful for men than women. The research coming out of the University of Queensland and presented at the Australian Institute of Family Studies Conference (2005) in Melbourne, found that men experience more stress than women in addressing these roles.

The authors claim that the erosion of traditional roles may be resulting in more stress for men. The study found that part-time workers had a better work–life balance compared to full-time workers. This might explain the fact that only 45 per cent of women in Australia with children under 6 are in the full-time workforce, this is lower than most other developed countries in the Western world. Commenting on the findings, Pru Goward, the then Sex Discrimination Commissioner in Australia, commented: 'The primary breadwinner model continues to shape men's identities and dominate the structure of their lives, often at the expense of family relationships.' These debates reflect the public–private dichotomy that has traditionally characterized working life.

Reflexivity, men and emotional labour

Masculinities have historically been linked with paid labour outside the home (Lupton and Barclay 1997; McDowell 2003). There is a long tradition in the Sociology of research into the public–private dichotomy (Sheller and Urry 2003), which has established strong gendered patterns in relation to home and work. Alongside this has been an understanding of distinct models of motherhood and fatherhood, with the latter being associated with breadwinning and instrumentality.

The last ten years have seen the emergence of new engaged discourses of fatherhood, with the emphasis on nurturing and more involved models of fatherhood (Cooper 2000; Dermott 2003). However, other writers (Coltrane 2004; La Rossa

1997) have shown that there is a significant gap between these new discourses of fatherhood and actual practices of fathering.

The crucial issue remains an economic one and the role of the father remains centrally located around work outside the home (Lewis 2000). It is hard to believe, but as Coltrane (2004) observes, the 'ideal professional worker' is still the man with the wife taking care of domestic responsibilities.

The low percentage (45 per cent) of women in Australia with a child under 6 in the full-time labour force appears to confirm this traditional model. In addition, men are often reluctant to take time off work to care for children for fear of appearing to be prioritizing home over work and thus not appearing sufficiently dedicated to career. The consensus in the literature (Cooper 2000; Kaufman and Uhlenberg 2000; Ranson 2001) as shown by Halford (2006: 387), indicates:

> that even amongst fathers who endorse new representations of fatherhood, the embodied practices of fathering children take place outside the time-space of the working day filled around long working hours and the demands of the workforce . . .

In a study of employed fathers who have been given the opportunity to work at home, Halford (2006) examines the implications of this for traditional models of fatherhood, but also considers the organizational impact of working at home in terms of the emergence of competing discourses of fatherhood, work and home.

The demographics of this group are not representative of the workforce as a whole. Felstead and Jewson (2000) note that those allowed to work from home are in a privileged minority, 60 per cent are male, at the highest end of the occupational spectrum and 58 per cent have dependent children. An additional factor, not discussed by Halford, is that while fathers are working from home, there is no indication that this is a direct benefit for women or mothers. It is not clear whether women remain at home under these circumstances or whether this encourages women to return to work.

Halford's (2006) study investigates home-working among a group of men with different ethnic backgrounds, who were all allowed the flexibility of home-working. She notes that the new time–space flexibility in fathers' involvement erased the structure of the working day and gave the man, in principle, an opportunity to increase his involvement in the routine aspects of parenting, for example, the school run and caring for sick children. Halford (ibid.: 391) notes that home-working has enabled fathers to integrate fathering practice with paid work.

Interestingly Halford (ibid.: 391–2) notes: 'Wives and partners were called on to police boundaries between home and work if children became too demanding or the workload was too heavy.' In fact, the crucial issue is, as Halford observes:

> critically these fathers were rarely responsible for the children during working hours, and if at all then only for brief periods of time. In all cases, mothers or other sources of care remained primary with the increase in father's involvement as an 'extra' on top of this.

The question has to be raised as to how valuable this intervention actually is in terms of the nature of emotional labour in the home. While these home-working fathers may have improved the quality of their fathering relationship, they relied on their partners or paid child-care to manage child-care responsibilities during working days and school holidays, so little change occurred in the pattern of arrangements in the home. It could be seen as another layer of work or responsibility in the daily routines.

From an organizational perspective, managers indicated that there was a concern that domestic responsibilities could distract employees during home-working, but the discussion proved difficult to have. Thus, as Halford (2006: 396) shows, home-working is not changing the public–private dichotomy significantly, nor apparently shifting the responsibilities in the household to encourage women to return to the public domain. This means that there is little potential in this mode for women to become more independent economically. In fact, Sheller and Urry (2003) argue that the distinction between public and private is untenable as both are hybridized along a range of dimensions.

Organizational context

The relationship between gender, identity and organizational frameworks, as developed in the literature, is now understood as more complex and diversified (Hassard *et al.* 2000; Kerfoot and Knights 1998; McDowell 1997; Simpson 2004; Simpson and Lewis 2005). Despite the dominance of hegemonic versions of masculinity, as McDowell (1997: 6) notes, both masculinity and femininity take multiple forms which are defined and constructed by organizational structures.

McDowell has shown the pervasiveness of US-based hegemonic practices in the securities industries in London financial services, as conveyed in the views of one of the women who had thought of working for Goldman Sachs before joining the British bank:

> I talked to all the American banks but I decided not to apply for them basically on the grounds that I don't like the culture. The very macho culture of, you know, 'We're all big swinging dicks here, if you come and be a bigger swinging dick, then that's fine, otherwise forget it.' Anyone who works less than 24 hours a day is, you know, a failure. I thought, I just don't want to do that with my life.

(ibid.:119)

Literature on the issues women continue to confront in the securities industry include overt and subtle forms of gender discrimination (Blair-Loy 2001, 2003; Blair-Loy and Jacobs 2003; Catalyst 2001; Costen 2001; Levin 2001; Roth 2001). In addition, senior finance-related jobs have become more competitive and demanding and, as Blair-Loy (2003: 174) indicates, the expectation is that high-ranking employees will put in very long hours, regardless of family obligations (Epstein *et al.* 1999; Williams 2000). As she shows, women lack support from a spouse at home

(Catalyst 2001; Hochschild 1997; Wajcman 1996). It is the processes operating in these organizations that help to sustain male domination of the industry.

The number of female brokers increased in the 1990s with women making up between 12–14 per cent of brokers in the industry (Securities Industry Association 1998). Evidence from Blair-Loy and Jacobs is that a sharply gendered division of labour characterizes the family life of brokers. The situation, while different in the UK and Europe, as a result of stricter regulation of working hours, still poses significant challenges for women in the financial sector.

Perrons (2004: 222) cites the case of Sandra Wood, a new mother and invest-ment analyst in the City of London. She expresses gratitude in being able to work just 10 hours a day (still in excess of EU regulations), although she and her fellow employees have 'voluntarily' opted out of the EU regulations on working hours. Her employer, in order to encourage long working hours, provides a range of serv-ices including: 'an on-site emergency creche, a designer café, restaurant, dentist, physiotherapist, doctor, nurse and gym available to all employees'. Perrons notes that firms generally have equal opportunity, family-friendly or work–life balance policies but high-level employees perceive that using them will damage their careers. In the case of Sandra Wood, she employed a nanny for 11 hrs a day, 5 days a week and was still left with between a half and three-quarters of her salary.

As both Perrons (2004) and McDowell (1997) have shown, these high-earn-ing mothers have complicated lives, working long hours and having little time. Their high incomes allow them to afford homes near the centres of cities where a range of service provision is available. Women, including ethnic minority women, can progress within organizations, although as McDowell has shown, most do not. However, as Perrons (2004: 1004) shows, some organizations are beginning to appreciate that they will have to be more flexible if they are to retain highly qualified women in senior positions. Citing a human resources manager at Micro-soft, who comments: 'We have top quality gourmet food always available and in the evening we run cookery classes . . . you also get *Waitrose Direct*, a grocery shopping service. Who wants to waste time pushing a supermarket trolley?'(Anita Chaudrey, 'Work Unlimited', the *Guardian*, 30 August 2000, cited in Perrons 2004).

The feminization of the workforce has inevitably impacted on organizational life and women in relatively small numbers are gaining access to elite, profes-sional, well-paid jobs. The changes that have taken place have had an unsettling effect on men and up to a point have led to a reassessment of male identity which is apparent from studies of household and family life. In addition, the role of the male as key provider in the home has been 'challenged by contemporary "femi-nized" forms of employment that offer different kinds of work, lower incomes and a lower degree of security' (Perrons 2004: 87).

Men in female-dominated occupations and emotional labour

The changing nature of work and organizational life and its impact on male identity are particularly apparent for men in female-dominated occupations. The question is, to what extent is the experience of men as regards emotional labour, differently experienced in female-dominated occupations? It is very apparent that there is a gender difference in the experience of men and women in female-dominated areas of work.

Conceptualizations of masculinity in the workplace have been well documented in the literature on entrepreneurialism. Indeed, it is clear from the literature on organizations and entrepreneurialism (du Gay 1996; Kerfoot and Knights 1998; Lewis 2004) that the discourses of entrepreneurialism and 'competitive masculinity' are very close, with a valorization and privileging of masculine values. Lewis (2004) in her study of female entrepreneurs, found that women in her study were not prepared to acknowledge the significance of gender as an issue in organizations. Other studies (Blair-Loy 2003; Brooks 2006; Piderit and Ashford 2003) have found a reluctance on the part of some women to recognize the significance of gender in organizational life.

Interestingly the response of men and women to finding themselves in minority positions in organizational life in entirely different. Lewis (2004) found that female entrepreneurs were keen to align themselves with their male colleagues, denying any difference in entrepreneurial behaviour and values. Thus 'by understanding their experience of entrepreneurship as the ability to abide by "universal"(male) standards of good business, some women hoped to evade "marking" by creating distance from any practices or values which may exclude or marginalise them' (Simpson and Lewis 2005: 26).

While the literature on 'token' women in organizations is quite extensive (Ely 1994; Kanter 1977; Simpson 1997, 2000), research on 'token' men in female-dominated occupations has been more limited (Bradley 1993; Heikes 1992; Lupton 2002; Williams 2000). The experiences and responses of token men in untypical occupations are interesting in understanding men's 'emotional' responses within occupations and to assess: 'how men manage any potential conflict between the "feminine" nature of the job and their gender identity' (Simpson 2004: 3).

While the concept of 'masculinity' is understood as a fractured and diversified concept (Alvesson 1998; Collinson and Hearn 1994; Kerfoot and Knights 1998), work is understood as central to masculine identity. Men in female-dominated organizations have been found to benefit from their 'token' status, unlike women who are seen to be disadvantaged. As Simpson (2004: 7) observes: 'Men working in non-traditional occupations have been found to benefit from their "token" status through the assumption of enhanced leadership and other skills and by being associated with a more careerist attitude to work (Heikes 1992).'

In addition, Bradley (1993) shows how male nurses ascend the hierarchy more quickly than their female counterparts. However, female-dominated occupations such as teaching, nursing and social work require a form of emotional labour that calls for special abilities which Hochschild (1983) maintains only women possess. As Heikes (1992) observes, this can call into question the suitability of men to work in these professions. Simpson (2004: 7) argues that these issues raise challenges about how men 'reconcile the feminine nature of their work with the demands of a hegemonically masculine gender regime'.They fear feminization and stigmatization (Lupton 2002) and adopt a number of strategies to restore their 'masculinity'. These strategies include: distancing themselves from female colleagues and interests, monopolizing positions of power, assuming positions of responsibility, carrying higher levels of pay and displaying careerist attitudes, including seeking positions of leadership.

However, a slightly different perspective is gained on men and emotional labour in female-dominated occupations in Simpson's (2004) study of librarians, primary school teachers, cabin crew and nurses. She shows how the motivations of men going into these occupations vary quite significantly, with some men finding themselves in these occupations as a short-term measure and the result of a lack of an alternative. In addition, Simpson found that the desire to assert a hegemonic masculinity into the positions in the form of seeking promotion was absent in many cases. For example, in the case of male nurses, several were unwilling to sacrifice time spent in clinical practice for the sake of seniority. As one male nurse commented: 'Men have come into nursing against the odds – so they don't want to be taken away from the job they enjoy and the reason they came into it in the first place' (ibid.: 13).

However, Simpson (ibid.: 16) also shows that most of the men recognized that their status as men gave them greater authority than their female counterparts: 'For example, male teachers were thought to be better at discipline and at handling difficult classes . . . Cabin crew argued that passengers felt safer in the presence of male crew because they were seen as having more authority.' While in some cases men did reassert a 'traditional masculinity', for example, male cabin crew claiming to have a 'cool [rational] head' in a crisis, most men gained enjoyment and satisfaction from the emotional labour elements of the job. In Simpson's study, in terms of sexual orientation, 14 men identified themselves as homosexual (1 librarian, 2 primary school teachers, 6 cabin crew and 5 nurses). There is no one clear-cut model of masculinity in regard to emotional labour in female-dominated occupations, but the nature of these occupations may attract men less concerned with traditionally conceived masculine hegemony and motivations.

More recently, Simpson (2009) has been looking at men in 'caring' occupations as a career choice and draws on the work of Williams (1993) who differentiated between three groups of men: (1) 'seekers' who actively sought female-dominated jobs; (2) 'finders' who were simply seeking alternative forms of work; and (3) 'leavers' who were in female jobs and left them. Simpson combines this categorization with an analysis of the gendered nature of caring occupations with an invisibility of caring occupations when occupied by women and an increased visibility and 'celebration' when such occupations are undertaken by men. Simpson's analysis shows how men engage in a range of strategies to make strategic use of difference in their choice of non-traditional occupations.

Conclusion

As has been shown in this chapter, emphasis is being given to the relationship between men, masculinity and emotional labour. The provision and expansion of services around emotional labour have applied mainly to executives and professionals, both single men and women and what Sassen (2003) has called 'professional households without wives'. Demographic factors have put greater emphasis on the issue of emotional labour as regards parenting responsibilities, and the demands of organizational life have changed the work–life balance and provided a range of services for employees.

This chapter reviewed a range of studies globally to indicate similar trends regarding masculinity and emotional labour. Despite the claims of some sociologists (Beck and Beck-Gernsheim 1996; Giddens 1992) of greater equity in the nature of relationships and more reflexivity regarding the conceptualization around emotion and intimacy, there appears to be little in this global analysis of masculinity to confirm this. This chapter has noted that there remains a significant gender gap in relation to emotional labour as shown in both the domestic and organizational context. The commercialization of intimacy as discussed in this book may assist women more than men to overcome the continuing obligations of emotional labour.

Conclusion

Ann Brooks

The emphasis and concentration of research into emotions, emotion work and emotional labour in the West are part of a shift in emphasis within the social sciences. This has been captured within a social constructivist approach to the study of emotions which has wide-ranging implications for understanding behaviour in different social and cultural contexts. These debates further opened up spaces for a consideration of reflexivity and identity in the 1990s linked in the work of Giddens (1992), Beck and Beck-Gernsheim (1996), among others, and to changing patterns of relationships and a democratization of intimacy.

These debates and the emergence of concepts such as emotional labour and emotion work are linked to debates around emotion in organizations and the growth of the service industry. As we have shown in this book, the seminal work of Arlie Hochschild, among others, significantly changed the landscape for understanding links between emotions and organizations and the work–life balance. However, these debates focused largely on the West with little or no application to Asia.

In this book, the authors have attempted to address the gap and to engage with gender emotions labour markets as well as with emotional labour debates in Asia as well as in the West. In the Introduction, the concepts of emotions, emotional labour and emotion work were explained and contextualized, showing the emergence of these concepts within a range of conceptual frameworks. The aims of the book were established in terms of how they relate to emotional labour and emotions more broadly. The framework for understanding gender within the social and cultural context of Asia was also examined.

In Chapter 1, Devasahayam provided an analysis of the relationship between globalization, labour force participation and the gender gap. She showed how women have been marginalized in five respects as a result of globalization: (1) in the formal sector of the economy; (2) in the gendered division of labour; (3) in the exploitative nature of multinational corporations; (4) in the double burden of work and family (although it is noted that is not solely an issue for women); and (5) in the negative effects of structural adjustment programmes of international financial institutions. She also showed how for women working in Asia, work is seen as complementary to family, but there is little recognition of what this involves. They are also seen as primarily secondary income earners, rather than primary income earners.

Devasahayam draws on a range of statistical data to highlight women's labour force participation as well as showing where and how the gender gap still persists. She points to a number of factors which impact on women's career opportunities across a number of countries. Her conclusions are that globalization is a 'double-edged sword' for Asian women, which has encouraged them to move into the labour force, but at the same time has led to a process of 'female proletarianization'. Devasahayam shows how governments in the region are disadvantaging themselves as a result of gender inequality, and some governments are attempting to remove some elements of discrimination against women. The Philippine and Taiwanese governments are making attempts in this direction. Additionally, women are working at national and transnational levels to challenge gender inequalities.

It is in this context that the discussion of parenting and emotional labour in Asia in Chapter 2 needs to be understood. In this chapter, Devasahayam and Brooks review the changing patterns of caregiving and emotional labour in Asia. Patterns of care are changing slowly and there are now a very large number of women occupying high-level professional positions especially in global cities such as Singapore, Hong Kong, Kuala Lumpur, Manilla, and Ho Chi Minh City (Saigon).

However, the emotional labour situation in most working-class and middle-class households is alleviated by 'maids' and while there may not have been a reassessment of emotional labour responsibilities, the burden of emotional labour has been transferred. There is something of a divide between urban/rural, middle-/working-class, educated/uneducated but overall the pattern is showing signs of change. This largely supports the political imperative to see women fully involved in productive labour, although the assumption is that they will still manage the emotional labour demands through the organization of a maid. In many of the countries of Southeast Asia, women are also making decisions to remain single, or delay marriage or even not have children at all (see Brooks 2010; Jones 2003, 2004).

The 'feminization of labour' globally is the result of the opening up of national borders and allowing the free flow of labour between countries. While the freeing of the global economy has offered opportunities, it has also produced global inequalities as women from countries in the developing world are encouraged to migrate and participate in different forms of labour overseas. While it is entirely incorrect to see migrant female labour as victims, it is equally true that female migrant labour is vulnerable to various forms of abuse, violence, and exploitation. In Chapter 3, Devasahayam examines both the feminization of labour and more particularly female migrant domestic labour. She examines what it means in terms of meeting emotional labour demands in receiving countries as well as managing their own emotional labour needs. She shows how the impulse to migrate is frequently the result of a desire on the part of women to escape abusive relationships and poverty. However, the costs to their own emotional labour needs are frequently difficult to reconcile.

Human rights has become an increasingly important issue in relation to female migrant labour particularly when it comes to rights of citizenship and human rights abuses. Devasahayam provides a backdrop to current UN human rights legislation in Chapter 4 in order to contextualize the issues. She shows how 'ambivalence towards the human rights discourse both in law and governance has been an underlying factor in the persistence of migrant rights abuses in Asia'. Devasahayam shows the human rights discourse is more of a problem with receiving countries than sending countries and the solution therefore frequently rests with individual states who lack 'political will'. She also indicates that despite the persistence of extensive abuses, many Asian women continue to work abroad because of perceived benefits. As Turner (2005: 204) comments, central to any human rights discourse is providing 'a moral framework of justice and universal human rights or capabilities such as the ability to live a normal life expectancy and be free from assault'. The issue for migrant women workers is that they are denied rights accorded to nationals. In many countries in the region, NGOs and religious organizations are responding to issues in the face of an apparent lack of action by governments. The matter is a serious and ongoing one with an expectation of urgent change.

The issue of emotional labour for different groups of workers is the focus of Chapter 5. In this chapter, Brooks analyses the emotional labour demands on professional women in the US and Asia-Pacific and considers their work–life balance. Brooks shows that emotional labour demands on professional women in the US and Asia need to be set in the context of different demographic patterns and cultural expectations and attitudes. The divorce rate is higher in the US and the demands made on professional women who are single parents pose challenges for these women in terms of their careers.

In Asia, the pressures are different in terms of demographic patterns and in terms of available support structures. Female migrant domestic labour has become an essential part of the emotional labour support in Asia with the success of professional women attributable to the availability of maids. Both in Asia and the West, these high-end professionals that Salazar Parreñas (2001a) describes as 'the servants of globalization' find themselves in work cultures and with emotional labour demands that are supported by low-paid female domestic labour from Asia and Central America. As Brooks shows, the significant added value provided by these workers is barely acknowledged by the receiving countries.

The servicing of these high-end professionals and the implications for the 'transnational community' of female domestic migrants are analysed by Brooks in Chapter 6. The emotional labour demands faced by this group of female migrant workers are examined as well as the violation of their human rights. Ong (2006) maintains that these workers are treated as 'biopolitical others' and this chapter provides suggestions for why they are abused and their rights violated. Brooks shows that these female migrant domestic workers suffer degradation from employers while attempting to handle the challenging situation of being separated from their family.

In the final chapter on men, masculinity and emotional labour, Brooks examines how men are located within emotional labour debates as fathers, spouses and in caring professions globally. Traditional conceptions of masculinity are clearly slow to change even in areas of work in which men are engaged and can be designated as 'female-dominated occupations'. This is an important area of investigation which has been under-researched in the area of emotional labour. It is only with a more fully researched field of masculinity and emotional labour will a comprehensive understanding of emotions and emotional labour be better understood.

In this book, the authors have explored issues emerging from emotions, emotional labour and emotion work in the very different cultural contexts of Asia and the West. Theoretical debates, empirical research, statistical data, media reports, policy documents and a wide range of global literature have been drawn on to review debates around the following: the global gender gap; Asian ideologies and cultural attitudes and practices; demographic change through patterns of divorce, singlehood and decline in fertility; patterns of migration and the 'feminization of migration'; human rights violations for migrant women; the experiences of professional women workers in Asia and the West; the division of emotional labour in executive households; 'the commercialization of intimate life'; parenting issues for women migrant workers; men, masculinity and emotional labour; and the changing pattern of men in the labour market.

The authors have drawn on paradigms used in the West to assess whether similar patterns are developing in Asia and the Asia-Pacific. While it is clear that there are parallels in attitudes of women towards careers and the need to address emotional labour demands, Asia is still characterized by resistance from men and traditional elements, if not from policy-makers. It is only where state policy (as in Singapore, Malaysia and Hong Kong) legislates to open its doors to female migrant labour to answer the emotional labour demands of women in Asia that the implications of the need for such labour are recognized. However, as we have seen, the response of the receiving countries has often been ambivalent and has resulted in human rights abuses of these workers. These abuses also operate at the level of the state when it comes to issues of citizenship rights (see Brooks and Wee 2010). In addition, Ali (2010: 5) raises the following questions which need further research:

Why in 2010 is there such a gap between the rights of women in the West and those in developing nations, especially in the Muslim world? . . . Poverty is one answer. But much of the oppression suffered by women outside the West is the outcome not of poverty but of principle: of values convictions, habits and traditions that are passing from generation to generation and enforced through persuasion, peer pressure, and too often force.

Bibliography

Adkins, L. (2002) *Revisions: Gender and Sexuality in Late Modernity*, Buckingham: Open University Press.

Ahmed, S., Castañeda, C., Fortier, A.-M. and Sheller, M. (2004) 'Introduction: uprootings/regroundings: questions of home and migration', in S. Ahmed, C. Castañeda and A.-M. Fortier (eds) *Uprootings/Regroundings: Questions of Home and Migration*, Oxford: Berg Publishers.

Aiyer, A., Devasahayam, T.W. and Yeoh, B.S.A. (2004) 'A clean bill of health: Filipinas as domestic workers in Singapore', *Asian and Pacific Migration Journal*, 13(1): 11–38.

Alexander, J. and Alexander, P. (2001) 'Markets as gendered domains: the Javanese *pasar*', in L.J. Seligmann (ed.) *Women Traders in Cross-Cultural Perspective: Mediating Identities, Marketing Wares*, Stanford, CA: Stanford University Press.

Ali, A.H. (2010) 'Women's rights coexist with wrongs', *The Weekend Australian*, March 13–14, Inquirer, 5.

Alvesson, M. (1998) 'Gender relations and identity at work: a case study of masculinities and femininities in an advertising agency', *Human Relations*, 51(8): 113–26.

Ang, S.L. (2006) 'Gender differentials in fields of study among graduates', *Singapore Statistics Newsletter*, Singapore: Singapore Department of Statistics.

Apodaca, C. (2002) 'The globalization of capital in East and Southeast Asia: measuring the impact on human rights standards', *Asian Survey*, 42(6): 883–905.

Appleton, S., Knight, J., Song, L. and Xia, Q. (2002) 'Labor retrenchment in China: determinants and consequences', *China Economic Review*, 13: 252–75.

Ashforth, B. and Humphrey, R. (1995) 'Emotion in the workplace: a reappraisal?' *Human Relations*, 48(2): 97–125.

Asian Development Outlook (2008a) 'Asia's labor migration dynamics'. Online Available HTTP: http://www.adb.org/Documents/books/ADO/2008/part020303.asp (accessed 8 November 2009).

Asian Development Outlook (2008b) 'Migration trends and directions'. Online Available HTTP: http://www.adb.org/Documents/Books/ADO/2008/part020302.asp (accessed 9 September 2008).

Asian Development Outlook (2009) 'Highlights-ADO 2009 update'. Online Available HTTP: http://www.adb.org/documents/books/ado/2009/update/highlights.pdf (accessed 12 January 2010).

Asian Human Rights Commission (2001) 'SINGAPORE: foreign workers in Singapore', Asian Human Rights Commission–Human Rights SOLIDARITY. Online Available HTTP: http://www.hrsolidarity.net/mainfile.php/1992vol01no01/1975/ (accessed 21 September 2005).

Asian Migration News (2009) 'Suicide among domestic workers,' 1–30 November. Online Available HTTP: http://www.smc.org.ph/amnews/amn0911/amn0911.htm#South_ Korea (accessed 22 January 2010).

Asis, M. (2003) 'International migration and families in Asia', in R. Iredale, C. Hawksley and S. Castles (eds) *Migration in the Asia Pacific: Population, Settlement and Citizenship Issues*, Cheltenham: Edward Elgar.

Asis, M., Huang, S. and Yeoh, B.S.A. (2004) 'When the light of the home is abroad: unskilled female migration and the Filipino family', *Singapore Journal of Tropical Geography*, 25(2): 198–215.

Austria, C.S.R. (2004) 'The church, the state and women's bodies in the context of religious fundamentalism in the Philippines', *Reproductive Health Matters*, 12(24): 96–103.

Ball, R. and Piper, N. (2002) 'Globalisation and regulation of citizenship: Filipino migrant workers in Japan', *Political Geography*, 21: 1013–34.

Battistella, G. and Conaco, M.C.G. (1998) 'The impact of labour migration on the children left behind: a study of elementary school children in the Philippines', *Sojourn: Journal of Social Issues in Southeast Asia*, 13(2): 220–41.

Baxter, J., Haynes, M. and Hewitt, J. 'Assessing change in the distribution of domestic labour over the lifecourse: pathways out of relationships', paper presented at the Research Conference, Melbourne, July 2007.

Beck, U. (1992) *Risk Society: Towards a New Modernity*, London: Sage.

Beck, U. (2000) *What is Globalization?* London: Polity Press.

Beck, U. and Beck-Gernsheim, E. (1996) *The Normal Chaos of Love*, Cambridge: Polity.

Beck, U., Giddens, A. and Lash, S. (1994) *Reflexive Modernization: Politics, Tradition and Aesthetics in the Modern Social Order*, Cambridge: Polity.

Becker, P.E. and Moen, P. (1999) 'Scaling back: dual-earner couples' work-family strategies', *Journal of Marriage and Family*, 61(4): 995–1007.

Bélanger, D. and Oudin, X. (2007) 'For better or worse?: Working mothers in late Vietnamese socialism', in T.W. Devasahayam and B.S.A. Yeoh (eds) *Working and Mothering in Asia: Images, Ideologies and Identities*, Singapore and Denmark: National University of Singapore Press and Nordic Institute of Asian Studies.

Beneria, L. (2008) 'The crisis of care, international migration, and public policy', *Feminist Economics*, 14(3): 1–21.

Benson. J. and Yukongdi, V. (2005) 'Asian women managers: participation, barriers and future prospects', *Asia Pacific Business Review*, 11(2): 283–91.

Berik, G. (2008) 'Growth with gender inequity: another look at East Asian development', in G. Berik, Y.V.D.M. Rodgers and A. Zammit (eds) *Social Justice and Gender Equality: Rethinking Development Strategies and Macroeconomic Policies*, London: Routledge.

Berik, G. and Rodgers, Y.V.D.M. (2008) 'Engendering development strategies and macroeconomic policies: what's sound and sensible?', in G. Berik, Y.V.D.M. Rodgers, and A. Zammit (eds) *Social Justice and Gender Equality: Rethinking Development Strategies and Macroeconomic Policies*, London: Routledge.

Berik, G., Rodgers, Y.V.D.M. and Zveglich, J.E. (2002) 'Does trade promote gender wage equity? Evidence from East Asia', Center for Economic Policy Analysis (CEPA) Working Paper 2002–14, New York.

Bernhardt, E.M. (1993) 'Fertility and employment', *European Sociological Review*, 9(1): 25–42.

Bhabha, J. and Coll, G. (eds) (1992) *Asylum Law and Practice in Europe and North America*, Washington, DC: Federal.

Blair-Loy, M. (2003) *Competing Devotions: Career and Family among Women Executives*, Cambridge, MA: Harvard University Press.

Blair-Loy, M. and Jacobs, J. (2003) 'Globalization, work hours and the care deficit among stockbrokers', *Gender and Society*, 17: 230–49.

Bosniak, L. (2002) 'Critical reflections on "citizenship" as a progressive aspiration', in J. Conaghan, R.M. Fischl and K. Klare (eds) *Labour Law in an Era of Globalization: Transformative Practices and Possibilities*, Oxford: Oxford University Press.

Bourdieu, P. (2000) *Distinction: A Social Critique of the Judgment of Taste*, trans. R. Nice, London: Routledge.

Bourdieu, P. (2001) *Masculine Domination*, Cambridge: Polity Press.

Bradley, H. (1993) 'Across the great divide', in C. Williams (ed.) *Doing Women's Work: Men in Non-Traditional Occupations*, London: Sage.

Brinton, M.C. (ed.) (2001) *Women's Working Lives in East Asia*, Stanford, CA: Stanford University Press.

Brinton, M.C. and Lee, S. (2001) 'Women's education and the labor market in Japan and South Korea', in M.C. Brinton (ed.) *Women's Working Lives in East Asia*, Stanford, CA: Stanford University Press.

Brodie, J. (2004) 'Introduction: globalization and citizenship beyond the national state', *Citizenship Studies*, 8(4): 323–32.

Brooks, A. (2003) 'The politics of location in Southeast Asia: intersecting tensions around gender, ethnicity, class and religion', *Asian Journal of Social Sciences*, 31(1): 86–106.

Brooks, A. (2006) *Gendered Work in Asian Cities: The New Economy and Changing Labour Markets*, Aldershot: Ashgate.

Brooks, A. (2008a) 'Reconceptualizing reflexivity and dissonance in professional and personal domains', *British Journal of Sociology*, 59(3): 539–59.

Brooks, A. (2008b) 'The commercialisation of intimacy: are women still left holding the baby?' University of Adelaide Research Tuesday Public Lecture Series, Adelaide, November 2008. Online Available HTTP: http://www.adelaide.edu.au/lifeimpactresearch/researchtuesday/anne_brooks.html (accessed 2 April 2009).

Brooks, A. (2010) *Social Theory in Contemporary Asia: Intimacy, Reflexivity and Identity*, London: Routledge.

Brooks, A. and Wee, L. (2008) 'Reflexivity and the transformation of gender identity: reviewing the potential for change in a cosmopolitan city', *Sociology*, 42(3): 503–21.

Brooks, A. and Wee, L. (2010) 'Sexual citizenship and the regulation of intimacy: citizenship as an ethical regime in cosmopolitan Asia', paper presented at the American Sociological Association 105th ASA Annual Conference, Towards a Sociology of Citizenship, Inclusion, Participation and Rights, Atlanta, GA, August.

Broomhill, R. and Sharp, R. (2004) 'The changing breadwinner model in Australia: a new gender order?', *Labour and Industry*, 15(2): 1–24.

Brubaker, R. (1992) *Citizenship and Nationhood in France and Germany*, Cambridge, MA: Harvard University Press.

Caldwell, J.C. and Caldwell, B.K. (2005) 'The causes of the Asian fertility decline: macro and micro approaches', *Asian Population Studies*, 1(1): 31–46.

CARAM Asia (2006) *State of Health of Migrants 2005: Access to Health*, Kuala Lumpur, Malaysia: Coordination of Action Research on AIDS and Mobility.

Carsten, J. (1995) 'Houses in Langkawi: stable structures or mobile homes?' in J. Carsten and S. Hugh-Jones (eds) *About the House: Lévi-Strauss and Beyond*, Cambridge: Cambridge University Press.

Carsten, J. (1997) *The Heat of the Hearth: The Process of Kinship in a Malay Fishing Community*, Oxford: Clarendon.

Castells, M. (2004) *The Network Society: A Cross-cultural Perspective*, Cheltenham: Edward Elgar.

Castles, S. and Davidson, A. (2000) *Citizenship and Migration: Globalization and the Politics of Belonging*, Basingstoke: Macmillan.

Castles, S. and Miller, M.J. (1998) *The Age of Migration: International Population Movements in the Modern World*, Basingstoke: Macmillan.

Castles, S. and Miller, M.J. (2003) *The Age of Migration*, New York: Guilford Press.

Catalyst (2001) *Women in Financial Services: The Word on the Street*, New York: Catalyst.

Chan, A. and Yeoh, B.S.A. (2002) 'Gender, family and fertility in Asia: an introduction', *Asia-Pacific Population Journal*, 17(2): 5–10.

Chan, A.H.-N. (2005) 'Live-in foreign domestic workers and their impact on Hong Kong's middle class families', *Journal of Family and Economic Issues*, 26(4): 509–28.

Chan, K.-B. and Wong, O.M.H. (2005) 'Introduction: private and public: gender, generation and family life in flux', *Journal of Family and Economic Issues*, 26(4): 447–64.

Chang, C.-F. (2009) 'Gender inequality in earnings in industrialized East Asia', Shorenstein APARC Dispatches. Online Available HTTP: http://aparcfellows.stanford.edu/news/february_2009_dispatch__gender_inequality_in_earnings_in_industrialized_east_asia_20090209/ (accessed 5 February 2010).

Chang, K.A. and Groves, J.M. (2000) 'Neither "saints" nor "prostitutes": sexual discourse in the Filipina domestic worker community in Hong Kong', *Women's Studies International Forum*, 23(1): 73–87.

Chaudhuri, S. (2010) 'Women's empowerment in South Asia and Southeast Asia: a comparative analysis', Munich Personal RePEc Archive, Paper No. 19686, Munich. Online Available HTTP: http://mpra.ub.uni-muenchen.de/19686/1/MPRA_paper_19686.pdf (accessed 6 February 2010).

Chaudrey, A. (2000) 'Work unlimited', *Guardian*, 30 August.

Cheah, W. (2006) 'Assessing criminal justice and human rights models in the fight against sex trafficking: a case study of the ASEAN region', *Essex Human Rights Review*, 3(1): 46–63.

Cheng, L. and Hsiung, P.-C. (1994) 'Women, export-oriented growth, and the state: the case of Taiwan', in J.D. Aberbach, D. Dollar and K.L. Sokoloff (eds) *The Role of the State in Taiwan's Development*, New York: M.E. Sharpe.

Cheng, S.-J.A. (1996) 'Migrant women domestic workers in Hong Kong, Singapore and Taiwan: a comparative analysis', *Asian and Pacific Migration Journal*, 5(1): 139–52.

Cheng, Y. and Chen, Y.-C. (2006) 'Foreign domestic workers in Taiwan: working conditions, psychological distress, and health status', paper presented at the International Society for Equity in Health (ISEqH) 4th International Conference, Adelaide, September.

Chew, P. (2004) 'Sons and daughters: benevolent patriarchy in Singapore', *NIASnytt*, 1: 6–7.

Chew, P. and Singam, C. (2004) 'Modern women, traditional wives', in A. Chin and C. Singam (eds) *Singapore Women Re-presented*, Singapore: Landmark Books.

Chia, S.Y. (2008) 'Demographic change and international labour mobility in Southeast Asia: issues, policies and implications for cooperation', in G. Hugo and S. Young (eds) *Labour Mobility in the Asia-Pacific Region*, Singapore: Institute of Southeast Asian Studies.

Chiang, L.-H.N. (2000) 'Women in Taiwan: linking economic prosperity and women's progress', in L. Edwards and M. Roces (eds) *Women in Asia: Tradition, Modernity and Globalization*, St. Leonards, NSW: Allen and Unwin.

Chin, C.B.N. (1998) *In Service and Servitude: Foreign Female Domestic Workers and the Malaysian Modernity Project*, New York: Columbia University Press.

Cholewinski, R., de Guchteneire, P. and Pécoud, A. (2009) *Migration and Human Rights: The United Nations Convention on Migrant Workers' Rights*, Cambridge: Cambridge University Press.

Chou, W.-C.G., Fosh, P. and Foster, D. (2005) 'Female managers in Taiwan: opportunities and barriers in changing times', *Asia Pacific Business Review*, 11(2): 251–66.

Clark, R., Ramsey, T.W. and Adler, E.S. (1991) 'Culture, gender and labor force participation: a cross-national study', *Gender & Society*, 5(1): 47–66.

Clarkberg, M. and Moen, P. (2001) 'Understanding the time squeeze, married couples, preferred and actual work-hour strategies', *American Behavioural Scientist*, 44(7): 115–36.

Clawen, A. (2002) 'Female labour migration to Bangkok: transforming rural-urban interactions and social networks through globalization', *Asia-Pacific Population Journal*, 17(3): 53–78.

Clegg, S., Dwyer, L., Gray, J., Kemp, S., Marceau, J. and O'Mara, E. (1995) 'Embryonic industries: leadership and management needs', in D. Midgley (ed.) *Enterprising Nation: Renewing Australia's Managers to Meet the Challenges of the Asia-Pacific Century*, Canberra: AGPS.

Clough, P. (2007) 'The affective turn: introduction', in P. Clough and J. Halley (eds) *The Affective Turn: Theorizing the Social*, Durham, NC: Duke University Press.

Clough, P. and Halley, J. (eds) (2007) *The Affective Turn: Theorizing the Social*, Durham, NC: Duke University Press.

Collinson, D. and Hearn, J. (1994) 'Naming men as men: implications for work, organization and management', *Gender, Work and Organization*, 1(1): 2–20.

Coltrane, S. (2004) 'Elite careers and family commitment: it's still about gender', *Annals of the American Academy*, 596: 214–20.

Coltrane, S. and Galt, J. (2000) 'The history of men's caring', in M.H. Meyer (ed.) *Care Work*, London: Routledge.

Conaghan, J., Fischl, R.M. and Klare, K. (eds) (2004) *Labour Law in an Era of Globalization: Transformative Practices and Possibilities*, Oxford: Oxford University Press.

Constable, N. (1997) *Maid to Order in Hong Kong: An Ethnography of Filipina Domestic Workers*, Ithaca, NY: Cornell University Press.

Constable, N. (2009) 'Migrant workers and the many states of protest in Hong Kong', *Critical Asian Studies*, 41(1): 143–64.

Convention and Protocol Relating to the Status of Refugees, 1 September 2007. Online Available HTTP: http://www.unhcr.org/3b66c2aa10.html (accessed 1 March 2010).

Cooke, F.L. (2007) ' "Husband's career first": renegotiating career and family commitment among migrant Chinese academic couples in Britain', *Work Employment and Society*, 21(1): 47–65.

Cooper, M. (2000) 'Being the "go-to-guy": fatherhood, masculinity and the organization of work in Silicon Valley', *Qualitative Sociology*, 23(4): 379–405.

Costen, W. (2001) 'Where are the women? Social closure in the financial services industry', unpublished dissertation, Washington State University.

Curran, S.R. (1995) 'Gender roles and migration: "good sons" vs. daughters in rural

Thailand', Working Paper 95-11, Center for Studies in Demography and Ecology, University of Washington, Seattle.

Custers, P. (1997) *Capital Accumulation and Women's Labour in Asian Economies*, London: Zed Books.

de Certeau, M. (1984) *The Practice of Everyday Life*, trans. S. Rendall, Berkeley, CA: University of California Press.

Dermott, E. (2003) 'The intimate father: defining paternal involvement', *Sociological Research Online*, 8(4). Online Available HTTP: http://socresearch.org.uk/8/4/dermott. html.

Devasahayam, T.W. (2001) 'Consumed with modernity and "tradition": food, women, and ethnicity in changing urban Malaysia', unpublished dissertation, Syracuse University.

Devasahayam, T.W. (2003a) 'Organisations that care: the necessity for an eldercare leave scheme for caregivers of the elderly in Singapore', Asian MetaCentre Research Papers, No. 10, National University of Singapore, Singapore. Online Available HTTP: http:// www.populationasia.org/Publications/ResearchPaper/AMCRP10.pdf (accessed 22 February 2010).

Devasahayam, T.W. (2003b) 'Empowering or enslaving?: What *adat* and *agama* mean for gender relations and domestic food production in Malay households in urban Malaysia', paper presented at Third International Convention of Asia Scholars (ICAS), Singapore, August.

Devasahayam, T.W. (2004) 'A culture of cherishing children: fertility trends of tertiary-educated Malay women in Malaysia', Working Papers, No. 23, Asia Research Institute, National University of Singapore, Singapore. Online Available HTTP: http://www.ari. nus.edu.sg/docs/wps04_023.pdf (accessed 5 October 2010).

Devasahayam, T.W. (2006a) '"As different as chalk and cheese?": Human rights and the spectrum of non-governmental organizations advocating for foreign domestic worker issues in Singapore', paper presented at History of Human Rights Interdisciplinary Workshop, Indiana, March.

Devasahayam, T.W. (2006b) 'Health risks: the experiences of female domestic workers in Hong Kong, Malaysia, Singapore, Taiwan and Thailand', paper presented at Emerging Population Issues in the Asian Pacific Region: Challenges for the 21st Century, Mumbai, December.

Devasahayam, T.W. (2009a) '"To call a spade a spade": gender and the new farming technologies in Southeast Asia', paper presented at Science Council of Asia Joint Project Workshop, Singapore, June.

Devasahayam, T.W. (2009b) 'Migrant labour in Asia: bracing for worse'. Online Available HTTP: http://opinionasia.com/MigrantLabourinAsia (accessed 25 November 2009).

Devasahayam, T.W. (2010) 'Placement and/or protection?: Singapore's labour policies and practices for temporary women migrant workers', *Journal of the Asia Pacific Economy*, 15(1): 45–58.

Devasahayam, T.W. and Yeoh, B.S.A. (eds) (2007) *Working and Mothering in Asia: Images, Ideologies and Identities*, Singapore and Denmark: National University of Singapore Press and Nordic Institute of Asian Studies.

DiQuinzio, P. (1999) *The Impossibility of Motherhood: Feminism, Individualism, and the Problem of Mothering*, New York: Routledge.

Dollar, D. and Gatti, R. (1999) 'Gender inequality, income, and growth: are good times good for women?' Policy Research Report on Gender and Development, Working Paper Series, No. 1, The World Bank. Online Available HTTP: http://darp.lse.ac.uk/frankweb/ courses/EC501/DG.pdf (accessed 19 January 2010).

Du Gay, P. (1996) *Consumption and Identity at Work*, London: Sage.

Dunn, D. and Skaggs, S. (1999) 'Gender and paid work in industrial nations', in J. S. Chafetz (ed.) *Handbook of the Sociology of Gender*, New York: Kluwer Publishers.

Ehrenreich, B. and Hochschild, A.R. (eds) (2003) *Global Woman: Nannies, Maids, and Sex Workers in the New Economy*, New York: Metropolitan Books.

Elmhirst, R. (2008) 'Multi-local livelihoods, natural resource management and gender in upland Indonesia', in B.P. Resurreccion and R. Elmhirst (eds) *Gender and Natural Resource Management: Livelihoods, Mobility and Interventions*, London: Earthscan.

Ely, R. (1994) 'The social construction of relationships among professional women at work', in M. Davidson and R. Burke (eds) *Women in Management: Current Research Issues*, London: Paul Chapman.

England, K. (1996) 'Mothers, wives, workers: the everyday lives of working mothers', in K. England (ed.) *Who Will Mind the Baby?: Geographies of Child Care and Working Mothers*, London: Routledge.

Epstein, C.F., Seron, C., Oglensky, B. and Saute, R. (1999) *The Part-time Paradox: Time Norms, Professional Lives, Family and Gender*, New York: Routledge.

Epstein, C.F., Seron, C., Oglensky, B., Saute, R. and Gever, M. (1995) 'Glass ceilings and open doors: women's advancement in the legal profession', *Fordham Law Review*, 64: 291–349.

Equal Opportunity for Women in the Workplace Agency (2006) *Paid Paternal Leave*, Canberra: Australian Government Publishing.

Fact Sheet No. 24, *The Rights of Migrant Workers*, International Convention on the Protection of the Rights of all Migrant Workers and Members of their Families (Art. 2, para. 1), adopted by General Assembly resolution 45/158 of I 8 December 1990. Online Available HTTP: http://www.agri-migration.eu/docs/The_rights_of_migrant_workers. doc (accessed 28 January 2010).

Falk, R. (2000) 'The decline of citizenship in an era of globalization', *Citizenship Studies*, 4(1): 5–17.

Felker, G.B. (2003) 'Southeast Asian industrialisation and the changing global production system', *Third World Quarterly*, 24(2): 255–82.

Felstead, A. and Jewson, N. (2000) *In Work at Home: Towards an Understanding of Home-working*, London: Routledge.

Fernail, A.B. (2005) 'Anaemia among migrant and non-migrant mothers in disadvantaged areas in the Visayas, the Philippines', in S. Jatrana, M. Toyota and B.S.A. Yeoh (eds) *Migration and Health in Asia*, London: Routledge.

Fernandez, I. (n.d.) 'Recognize domestic work as work with one paid day off to drastically reduce violence against DWs'. Online Available HTTP: http://www.tenaganita.net/index. php?option=com_content&task=view&id=261&Itemid=51 (accessed 28 January 2010).

Fineman, S. (2000) *Emotion in Organizations*, London: Sage.

Fineman, S. (2005) 'Appreciating emotions at work: paradigm tensions', *International Journal of Work, Organization and Emotion*, 1(1): 4–19.

Fisher, C.D. and Ashkanasy, N.M. (2000) 'The emerging role of emotions in work life: an introduction', *Journal of Organizational Behaviour*, 21(2): 123–9.

Fisher, M. (2002) 'Wall Street women's "Her Stories" in late financial corporate capitalism', in K. Lipartito and D. Sicilia (eds) *Constructing Corporate America: History, Politics, Culture*, New York: Oxford University Press.

Fitzpatrick, J. and Kelly, K.R. (1998–1999) 'Gendered aspects of migration: law and the female migrant', *Hastings International and Comparative Law Review*, 22: 47–112.

Fontana, M. (2009) 'Implications of current trade policies for gender equality', paper presented at the Expert Group Meeting on the Impact of the Implementation of the Beijing Declaration and Platform for Action on the Achievement of the Millennium Development Goals, Geneva, November.

Fortier, A.-M. (2004) 'Making home: queer migrations and motions of attachment', in S. Ahmed, C. Casteñada and A.-M. Fortier (eds) *Uprootings/Regroundings: Questions of Home and Migration*. Oxford: Berg Publishers.

Frost, P.J. (2004) 'Handling toxic emotions: new challenges for leaders and their organization', *Organizational Dynamics*, 33(2): 111–117.

Frost, P.J. (2007) *Toxic Emotions at Work and What you Can Do About Them*. Harvard: Harvard Business School Press.

Gallagher, A. (2005) 'Violence against and trafficking in women as symptoms of discrimination: the potential of CEDAW as an antidote', Gender and Development Discussion Paper Series No. 17, Bangkok: Economic and Social Commission for Asia and the Pacific.

Gamburd, M.R. (2000) 'Nurture for sale: Sri Lankan housemaids and the work of mothering', in K.M. Adams and S. Dickey (eds) *Home and Hegemony: Domestic Service and Identity Politics in South and Southeast Asia*, Ann Arbor, MI: University of Michigan Press.

Garey, A.I. (1999) *Weaving Work and Motherhood*, Philadelphia, PA: Temple University Press.

Gender and Development InBrief (2005) 'Gender & migration: an overview', Issue 16 October. Online Available HTTP: http://www.bridge.ids.ac.uk//bridge/Docs/InBrief16.pdf (accessed 24 November 2009).

Gereffi, G. and Sturgeon, T.J. (2004) 'Globalization, employment and economic development: a briefing paper'. Online Available HTTP: http://www.soc.duke.edu/sloan_2004/Docs/Briefing.pdf (accessed 15 February 2010).

Gheradi, S. (1995) *Gender, Symbolism and Organizational Culture*, London: Sage.

Giddens, A. (1991) *Modernity and Self Identity: Self and Society in the Late Modern Age*, Cambridge: Polity.

Giddens, A. (1992) *The Transformation of Intimacy: Sexuality, Love and Eroticism in Modern Societies*, Cambridge: Polity.

Gill, L. (1994) *Precarious Dependencies: Gender, Class, and Domestic Service in Bolivia*, New York: Columbia University Press.

Glass, J. (2000) 'Envisioning the integration of work and family: toward a kinder, gentler workplace', *Contemporary Sociology*, 29: 129–43.

Global Commission on International Migration (2005) *Migration in an Interconnected World: New Directions for Action*, Report of the Global Commission on International Migration, Geneva: Global Commission on International Migration.

Global Migration Group (2008) *International Migration and Human Rights: Challenges and Opportunities on the Threshold of the 60th Anniversary of the Universal Declaration of Human Rights*. Online Available HTTP: http://www.globalmigrationgroup.org/pdf/Int_Migration_Human_Rights.pdf (accessed 14 February 2010).

Go, S.P. (2002) 'Remittances and international labour migration: impact on the Philippines', paper presented for the Metropolis Interconference Seminar on Immigrants and Homeland, Dubrovnik, May.

Grant, S. (2005a) 'International migration and human rights', paper prepared for the Policy Analysis and Research Programme of the Global Commission on International Migration. Online Available HTTP: http://www.gcim.org/attachements/TP7.pdf (accessed 14 February 2010).

Grant, S. (2005b) 'Migrants' human rights: from the margins to the mainstream'. Online Available HTTP: http://www.migrationinformation.org/Feature/display.cfm?ID=291 (accessed 1 March 2010).

Greco, M. and Stenner, P. (eds) (2008) *Emotions: A Social Science Reader*, London: Routledge.

Gurowitz, A. (1999) 'Mobilizing international norms: domestic actors, immigrants, and the Japanese state', *World Politics*, 51(3): 413–45.

Gurowitz, A. (2000) 'Migrant rights and activism in Malaysia: opportunities and constraints', *Journal of Asian Studies*, 59(4): 863–88.

Halford, S. (2006) 'Collapsing the boundaries? Fatherhood, organization and home-working', *Gender, Work and Organization*, 13(4): 383–402.

Hannerz, U. (1990) 'Cosmopolitans and locals in world culture', in M. Featherstone (ed.) *Global Culture: Nationalism, Globalization and Modernity*, London: Sage.

Hassard, J., Holliday, R. and Willmott, H. (eds) (2000) *Body and Organization*, London: Sage.

Hatcher, C. (2003) 'Refashioning passionate manager: gender at work', *Gender, Work and Organization*, 10(4): 391–412.

Haughton, J. (1997) 'Falling fertility in Vietnam', *Population Studies*, 51(2): 203–11.

Hays, S. (1996) *The Cultural Contradictions of Motherhood*, New Haven, CT: Yale University Press.

Hearn, J. (1994) 'Changing men and changing management: social change, social research and social action', in M. Davidson and R. Burke (eds) *Women in Management: Current Research Issues*, London: Paul Chapman.

Heikes, J. (1992) 'When men are in the minority: the case of men in nursing', *The Sociological Quarterly*, 32(3): 389–401.

Held, D. (1999) 'The transformation of political community: rethinking democracy in the context of globalization', in I. Shapiro and C. Hacker-Cordón (eds) *Democracy's Edges*, Cambridge: Cambridge University Press.

Hensman, R. (1996) 'A feminist movement in Sri Lanka: the potential and the necessity', *Contemporary South Asia*, 5(1): 67–74.

Herdt, G. (ed.) (1997) *Sexual Cultures and Migration in the Era of AIDS: Anthropological and Demographic Perspectives*, Oxford: Clarendon Press.

Heyzer, N. (1986) *Working Women in South-east Asia: Development, Subordination and Emancipation*, London: Open University Press.

Hilsdon, A.-M. (2007) 'The musician, the masseuse and the manager: sexy mothers in Sabah', in T.W. Devasahayam and B.S.A. Yeoh (eds) *Working and Mothering in Asia: Images, Ideologies and Identities*, Singapore and Denmark: National University of Singapore Press and Nordic Institute of Asian Studies.

Hing A.Y., Karim, N.S. and Talib, R. (eds) (1984) *Women in Malaysia*, Petaling Jaya: Pelanduk Publications.

Hippert, C. (2002) 'Multinational corporations, the politics of the world economy, and their effects on women's health in the developing world: a review', *Health Care for Women International*, 23(8): 861–69.

Hirao, K. (2001) 'Mothers as the best teachers: Japanese motherhood and early childhood education', in M.C. Brinton (ed.) *Women's Working Lives in East Asia*, Stanford, CA: Stanford University Press.

Hirao, K. (2007) 'Contradictions in maternal roles in contemporary Japan', in T.W. Devasahayam and B.S.A. Yeoh (eds) *Working and Mothering in Asia: Images, Ideologies and*

Identities, Singapore and Denmark: National University of Singapore Press and Nordic Institute of Asian Studies.

Hochschild, A.R. (1983) *The Managed Heart: Commercialization of Human Feeling*, Berkeley, CA: University of California Press.

Hochschild, A.R. (1989) 'The managed heart', in J.J. Macionis and N.V. Benokraitis (eds) *Seeing Ourselves: Classic, Contemporary, and Cross-cultural Readings in Sociology*, Englewood Cliffs, NJ: Prentice Hall.

Hochschild, A.R. (1990) *The Second Shift: Working Parents and the Revolution at Home* (with A. Machung), London: Piatkus.

Hochschild, A.R. (1993) 'Preface', in S. Fineman (ed.) *Emotions in Organizations*, London: Sage.

Hochschild, A.R. (1997) *The Time Bind: When Work Becomes Home and Home Becomes Work*, New York: Metropolitan Books.

Hochschild, A.R. (2003a) *The Commercialization of Intimate Life*, Berkeley, CA: The University of California Press.

Hochschild, A.R. (2003b) 'Love and gold', in B. Ehrenreich and A.R. Hochschild (eds) *Global Woman: Nannies, Maids, and Sex Workers in the New Economy*, New York: Metropolitan Books.

Hochschild, A.R. (2005) ' "Rent a mom" and other services: markets, meanings and emotions', *International Journal of Work, Organization and Emotion*, 1: 74–86.

Hochschild, A.R. (2008) 'Emotion work, feeling rules and social structure', Extracted in M. Greco and P. Stenner (eds) *Emotions: A Social Science Reader*, London: Routledge.

Holroyd, E.A., Molassiotis, A. and Taylor-Pilliae, R.E. (2001) 'Filipino domestic workers in Hong Kong: health related behaviours, health locus of control and social support', *Women & Health*, 33(1/2): 181–205.

Hondagneu-Sotelo, P. (2001) *Doméstica: Immigrant Workers Cleaning and Caring in the Shadows of Affluence*, Berkeley, CA: University of California Press.

Hondagneu-Sotelo P. and Avila, E. (1997) ' "I'm here, but I'm there": the meanings of Latina transnational motherhood', *Gender & Society*, 11(5): 548–71.

Huang, S. and Yeoh, B.S.A. (1996) 'Ties that bind: state policy and migrant female domestic helpers in Singapore', *Geoforum* 27(4): 479–93.

Huang, S. and Yeoh, B.S.A. (1998) 'Beyond the household: strategizing childcare in Singapore', *Asian Profile*, 25(3): 193–209.

Huang, S. and Yeoh, B.S.A. (2003) 'The difference gender makes: state policy and contract migrant workers in Singapore', *Asian and Pacific Migration Journal*, 12(1–2): 75–97.

Huang, S., Yeoh, B.S.A. and Lam, T. (2008) 'Asian transnational families in transition: the liminality of simultaneity', *International Migration*, 46(4): 3–13.

Huang, S., Yeoh, B.S.A. and Straughan, P. (2007) 'Sustaining the household in a globalizing world: the gendered dynamics of business travel', *Philippine Studies*, 55(2): 243–74.

Hugo, G. (2002) 'Effects of international migration on the family in Indonesia', *Asian and Pacific Migration Journal*, 11(1): 13–46.

Huguet, J.W. (2003) 'International migration and development: opportunities and challenges for poverty reduction', in Fifth Asian and Pacific Population Conference, Asian Population Studies Series, No. 158, New York: United Nations.

Huguet, J.W. and Punpuing, S. (2005) *International Migration in Thailand*, Bangkok: International Organization for Migration.

Hull, T.H. (1994) 'Fertility decline in the New Order period: the evolution of population policy, 1965–1990', in H. Hill (ed.) *Indonesia's New Order: The Dynamics of Socio-Economic Transformation*, Sydney: Allen and Unwin.

Hull, T. (2002) 'The marriage revolution in Indonesia', paper presented at the Annual Meeting of the Population Association of America, Atlanta, GA.

Human Rights Watch (2005) 'Malaysia: migrant workers fall prey to abuse', 18 May. Online Available HTTP: http://www.hrw.org/en/news/2005/05/16/malaysia-migrant-workers-fall-prey-abuse (accessed 25 January 2010).

Huppatz, K. (2009) 'Reworking Bourdieu's "capital": feminine and female capitals in the field of paid caring work', *Sociology* 43: 45–66.

Illouz, E. (1997) 'Who will take care of the caretaker's daughter? Towards a sociology of happiness in the era of reflexive modernity', *Theory, Culture and Society*, 14(1): 31–66.

International Labour Organization (1998) 'Unit 2: Gender issues in the world of work: Emerging gender issues in the Asia Pacific region'. Online Available HTTP: http://www.ilo.org/public/english/region/asro/mdtmanila/training/unit2/migngpex.htm (accessed 17 January 2010).

International Labour Organization (2003) *Global Employment Trends Model*, Geneva, Switzerland: International Labour Organization. Online Available HTTP: www.ilo.org/public/english/employment/strat/download/trends.pdf (accessed 23 July 2007).

International Labour Organization (2005) *Women's Employment: Global Trends, ILO Responses*, paper presented at the 49th Session of the Commission on the Status of Women, New York. Online Available HTTP: www.ilo.org/.../docs/RES/399/F1503666968/Womens%20Employment%20%20Global%20Trends%20and%20ILO%20Respon.pdf (accessed 23 July 2007).

International Labour Organization (2009a) *Global Employment Trends for Women*, Geneva: International Labour Organization. Online Available HTTP: http://www.ilo.org/public/libdoc/ilo/P/09275/09275(2009).pdf (accessed 5 October 2010).

International Labour Organization (2009b) 'National labour migration policy for Sri Lanka launched', 26 May. Online Available HTTP: http://www.ilo.org/public/english/protection/migrant/info/mpolicy_srilanka.htm (accessed 25 November 2009).

International Labour Organization (2010) *Global Employment Trends*, Geneva: International Labour Office.

International Organization for Migration (2000) *Combating Trafficking in South-east Asia: A Review of Policy and Programme Responses*, Report prepared for IOM by Annuska Derks, Geneva: International Organization for Migration.

International Organization for Migration (2008) *Situation Report on International Migration in East and South-east Asia*, Bangkok: International Organization for Migration.

International Trade Union Confederation (2008) *The Global Gender Pay Gap*. Online Available HTTP: http://www.ituc-csi.org/IMG/pdf/gap-1.pdf (accessed 10 January 2010).

International Women's Rights Action Watch Asia Pacific, Global Alliance Against Traffic in Women, and Coordination of Action Research on AIDS and Mobility (2009) 'Round-table on using CEDAW to protect the rights of women migrant workers and trafficked women in South and Southeast Asia'. Online Available HTTP: http://www.gaatw.org/publications/Roundtable_on_Migration_and_Trafficking_report.pdf (accessed 1 March 2010).

Isin, E.F. and Turner, B.S. (2008) 'Investigating citizenship: an agenda for citizenship stud-ies', in E.F. Isin, P. Nyers and B.S. Turner (eds) *Citizenship between Past and Future*, New York: Routledge.

Jacobs, J. and Gerson, K. (2001) 'Overworked individuals or overworked families: explain-ing trends in work, leisure and family time', *Work and Occupations*, 28(1): 40–63.

Jagger, A.M. (2001) 'Is globalization good for women?' *Comparative Literature*, 53(4): 298–314.

Jatrana, S., Toyota, M. and Yeoh, B.S.A. (eds) (2005) *Migration and Health in Asia*, London: Routledge.

Jolly, S. and Reeves, H. (2005) *Gender and Migration: Overview Report*, Brighton: Bridge Institute of Development Studies.

Jomo, K.S. (2009) 'Export-oriented industrialisation, female employment and gender wage equity in East Asia', *Economic and Political Weekly*, 44(1): 41–9.

Jomo, K.S. and Chen, Y.C. (1997) *Southeast Asia's Misunderstood Miracle: Industrial Policy and Economic Development in Thailand, Malaysia and Indonesia*, Boulder, CO: Westview Press.

Jones, G. (2002) 'The changing Indonesian household', in K. Robinson and S. Bessell (eds) *Women in Indonesia: Gender, Equity and Development*, Singapore: Institute of Southeast Asian Studies.

Jones, G. (2003) 'The "flight from marriage" in South-east and East Asia', *Asian Meta-Centre Research Paper Series*, No. 11, National University of Singapore, Singapore. Online Available HTTP: http://www.populationasia.org/Publications/RP/AMCRP11.pdf (accessed 10 February 2010).

Jones, G. (2004) 'Not "when to marry" but "whether to marry"', in G.W. Jones and K. Ramdas (eds) *(Un)tying the Knot: Ideal and Reality in Asian Marriage*, Singapore: Asia Research Institute and National University of Singapore.

Jones, G. (2007) 'Delayed marriage and very low fertility in Pacific Asia', *Population and Development Review*, 33(3): 453–78.

Jones, G. (2009a) 'Women, marriage and family in Southeast Asia', in T.W. Devasahayam (ed.) *Gender Trends in Southeast Asia: Women Now, Women in the Future*, Singapore: Institute of Southeast Asian Studies.

Jones, G. (2009b) 'Recent fertility trends, policy responses and fertility prospects in low fertility countries of East and Southeast Asia', paper prepared for the Expert Group Meeting on Recent and Future Trends in Fertility, United Nations Population Division, New York, December.

Jones, G. and Shen, H-H. (2008) 'International marriage in East and Southeast Asia: trends and research emphases', *Citizenship Studies*, 12(1): 9–25.

Jones, G., Straughan, P.T. and Chan, A. (2009a) 'Very low fertility in Pacific Asian countries: causes and policy responses', in G. Jones, P.T. Straughan and A. Chan (eds) *Ultra-low Fertility in Pacific Asia: Trends, Causes and Policy Issues*, New York: Routledge.

Jones, G., Straughan, P.T. and Chan, A. (2009b) 'Fertility in Pacific Asia: looking to the future', in G. Jones, P.T. Straughan and A. Chan (eds) *Ultra-low Fertility in Pacific Asia: Trends, Causes and Policy Issues*, New York: Routledge.

Kang, H.-R. and Rowley, C. (2005) 'Women in management in South Korea: advancement or retrenchment?', *Asia Pacific Business Review*, 11(2): 213–31.

Kannan, K.P. and Hari, K.S. (2002) 'Kerala's gulf connection: remittances and their macroeconomic impact', in K.C. Zachariah, K.P. Kannan and S.I. Rajan (eds) *Kerala's Gulf Connection*, Thiruvananthapuram, Kerala: Centre for Development Studies.

Kanter, R. (1997) *Men and Women of the Corporation*, New York: Basic Books.

Karim, W.J. (1995) 'Introduction: genderising anthropology in Southeast Asia', in W.J. Karim, (ed.) *'Male' and 'Female' in Developing Southeast Asia*, Oxford: Berg Publishers.

Kaufman, G. and Uhlenberg, P. (2000) 'The influence of parenthood on work effort of married men and women', *Social Forces*, 78(3): 931–47.

Kaur, A. (2004) 'Economic globalisation, trade liberalisation and labour-intensive export manufactures: an Asian perspective', in A. Kaur (ed.) *Women Workers in Industrialising Asia: Costed, Not Valued*, New York: Palgrave Macmillan.

Kaur, A. (2007) 'International labour migration in Southeast Asia: governance of migration and women domestic workers', *Intersections: Gender, History and Culture in the Asian Context*, 15. Online Available HTTP: http://intersections.anu.edu.au/issue15/kaur.htm (accessed 4 January 2010).

Kawewe, S.M. and Dibie, R. (2000) 'The impact of economic structural adjustment programs [ESAPs] on women and children: implications for social welfare in Zimbabwe', *Journal of Sociology and Social Welfare*, 27(4): 79–107.

Kearney, A.T. (2007) 'Hong Kong, Jordan, and Estonia debut among the top 10 in expanded ranking of the world's most globalized countries', 22 October. Online Available HTTP: http://www.atkearney.com/index.php/News-media/hong-kong-jordan-and-estonia-debut-among-the-top-10-in-expanded-ranking-of-the-worlds-most-globalized-countries. html (accessed 10 February 2010).

Kerfoot, D. and Knights, D. (1998) 'Managing masculinity in contemporary organizational life', *Organization*, 5(1): 7–26.

Khondker, H. (2009) 'Socio-economic development and gender empowerment in the ASEAN region', *Gender Perspectives*, 1(2): 1–3, Singapore: Institute of Southeast Asian Studies. Online Available HTTP: http://www.iseas.edu.sg/GenderEbulletin-Dec2009. pdf (accessed 8 February 2010).

Kimmel, M. (ed.) (2000) *The Gendered Society Reader*, Oxford: Oxford University Press.

'Know Your Rights', G.A. res. 217A (III), U.N. Doc A/810 at 71 (1948). Online Available HTTP: http://www.udhr.org/udhr/default.htm (accessed 1 March 2010).

Koller, V. (2004) 'Business women and war metaphors: possessive, jealous and pugnacious', *Journal of Sociolinguistics*, 18(1): 4–12.

Komnas Perempuan and Solidaritas Perempuan/CARAM Indonesia (2006) *Indonesian Migrant Domestic Workers: Their Vulnerabilities and New Initiatives for the Protection of their Rights*, Indonesia: Komnas Perempuan and Solidaritas Perempuan/CARAM Indonesia.

Kong, L.L.L. and Chan, J.S. (2000) 'Patriarchy and pragmatism: ideological contradictions in state policies', *Asian Studies Review*, 24(4): 501–31.

Koslowski, R. (2000) *Migrants and Citizens: Demographic Change in the European State System*, Ithaca, NY: Cornell University Press.

Lai, A.E. and Huang, S. (2004) 'The other chief executive officer: homemaking as a sequencing strategy and career project among married Chinese women in Singapore', in L.L. Thang and W.-H. Yu (eds) *Old Challenges, New Strategies: Women, Work and Family in Contemporary Asia*, Leiden: Brill.

La Rossa, F. (1997) *The Modernization of Fatherhood: A Social and Political History*, Chicago: University of Chicago Press.

Latif, A. (2002) 'To veil or not to veil?', *The Straits Times*, Singapore, 16 March.

Laumann, E., Michael, R., Michaels, S. and Gagnon, J. (1994) *The Social Organization of Sexuality*, Chicago: University of Chicago Press.

Lauser, A. (2008) 'Philippine women on the move: marriage across borders', *International Migration*, 46(4): 85–108.

Law, L. (2003) 'Sites of transnational activism: Filipino non-government organisations in Hong Kong', in B.S.A. Yeoh, P. Teo and S. Huang (eds) *Gender Politics in the Asia-Pacific Region*, London: Routledge.

Law, L. and Nadeau, K. (1999) 'Globalization, migration and class struggles: NGO mobilization for Filipino domestic workers', *Kasarinlan Philippine Journal of Third World Studies*, 14(3): 51–68.

Lazar, M.M. (1999) 'Family life advertisements: and the narrative of heterosexual sociality', in P.G.L. Chew and A. Kramer-Dahl (eds) *Reading Culture: Textual Practices in Singapore*, Singapore: Times Academic Press.

Lee, E. (2011) 'A lawyer's perspective on how divorcees view the Women's Charter', in T.W. Devasahayam (ed.) *The Singapore Women's Charter: Roles, Responsibilities and Rights in Marriage*, Singapore: Institute of Southeast Asian Studies.

Lee, J.-W. (2009) 'Asia's delicate balancing act in globalization', *The Straits Times*, 22 September. Online Available HTTP: http://www.adb.org/Documents/Op-Ed/2009/oped-02.asp (accessed 5 February 2010).

Lee, J., Campbell, K. and Chia, A. (1999) *The 3 Paradoxes: Working Women in Singapore*, Singapore: Association of Women for Action and Research.

Levin, P. (2001) 'Gendering the market: temporality, work and gender and the National Futures Exchange', *Work and Occupations*, 29: 112–30.

Lewis, C. (2000) *A Man's Place in the Home: Fathers and Families in the UK*, York: Joseph Rowntree Foundation.

Lewis, P. (2004) 'Using conflict to highlight the gendered nature of entrepreneurship: the case of the career woman entrepreneur', paper presented at the British Academy of Management Conference.

Lewis, P. and Simpson, R. (eds) (2007) *Gendering Emotions in Organizations*, New York: Palgrave Macmillan.

Litt, J.S. and Zimmerman, M.K. (2003) 'Guest editors' introduction: global perspectives on gender and carework: an introduction', *Gender & Society*, 17: 156–65.

Liu, A.Y.C. (2004) 'Sectoral gender wage gap in Vietnam', *Oxford Development Studies*, 32(2): 225–39.

Lovell, T. (2000) 'Thinking feminism with and against Bourdieu', in B. Fowler (ed.) *Reading Bourdieu on Society and Culture*, Oxford: Blackwell.

Luong, H.V. (2003) 'Gender relations: ideologies, kinship practices, and political economy', in H.V. Luong (ed.) *Postwar Vietnam: Dynamics of a Transforming Society*, Singapore and Lanham, MD: Institute of Southeast Asian Studies and Rowman and Littlefield.

Lupton, B. (2002) 'Maintaining masculinities: men who do women's work', *British Journal of Management*, 11, S33–48.

Lupton, D. and Barclay, L. (1997) *Constructing Fatherhood*, London: Sage.

Lyons-Lee, L. (1998) 'The "graduate woman" phenomenon: changing constructions of the family in Singapore', *Sojourn: Journal of Social Issues in Southeast Asia*, 13(2): 309–27.

Mackie, V. (2001) 'The language of globalization, transnationality and feminism', *International Feminist Journal of Politics*, 3(2): 180–206.

Maher, J.M., Lindsay, J. and Franzway, S. (2008) 'Time, caring labour and social policy: understanding the family time economy in contemporary families', *Work Employment and Society*, 22(3): 547–58.

Marchand, M.H. and Runyan A.S. (eds) (2000) *Gender and Global Restructuring*, London: Routledge

Marsh, I., Blondel, J. and Inoguchi, T. (eds) (1999) *Democracy, Governance and Economic Performance: East and Southeast Asia*, Tokyo: United Nations University Press.

Marshall, T.H. (1963) *Class, Citizenship and Social Class*, New York: Doubleday.

Martin, J., Knopoff, K. and Beckman, C. (1998) 'An alternative to bureaucratic, impersonal and emotional labour at the Body Shop', *Administrative Science Quarterly*, 43: 429–69.

Massumi, B. (2002) *Parables of the Virtual: Movement, Affect, Sensation*, Durham, NC: Duke University Press.

Mathiaparanam, B. (2008) 'Status of women in Singapore and trends in Southeast Asia', *Panorama: Insights into Southeast Asian and European Affairs*, 1: 37–49.

Matsui, Y. (1999) *Women in the New Asia*, London: Zed Books.

McCall, L. (1992) 'Does gender fit? Bourdieu, feminism and conceptions of the social order', *Theory and Society*, 21(6): 837–67.

McDonald, P. (2002) 'Below replacement fertility in Asia: determinants and consequences', paper presented at the International Workshop on Fertility Decline, Below Replacement Fertility and the Family in Asia: Prospects, Consequences and Policies, Singapore, April.

McDonald, P. (2009) 'Explanations of low fertility in East Asian: a comparative perspective', in G. Jones, P.T. Straughan and A. Chan (eds) *Ultra-low Fertility in Pacific Asia: Trends, Causes and Policy Issues*, New York: Routledge.

McDowell, L. (1997) *Capital Culture: Gender at Work in the City*, Oxford: Blackwell.

McDowell, L. (2003) *Redundant Masculinities: Employment Change and White Working Class Youth*, Oxford: Blackwell.

McNay, L. (1999) 'Gender, habitus and field: Pierre Bourdieu and the limits of reflexivity', *Theory, Culture and Society*, 16(1): 95–117.

McNay, L. (2000) *Gender and Agency: Reconfiguring the Subject in Feminist and Social Theory*, Cambridge: Polity.

McNay, L. (2008) *Against Recognition*, Cambridge: Polity.

Meyer, M.H. (2000) *Care Work*, New York: Routledge.

Migration News (1996) 'Philippine maid returns home'. Vol. 3, No. 9. Online Available HTTP: http://migration.ucdavis.edu/MN/more.php?id=1037_0_3_0 (accessed 24 November 2009).

Mills, M.B. (2003) 'Gender and inequality in the global labor force", *Annual Review of Anthropology*, 32: 41–62.

Mirchandani, K. (2003) 'Challenging racial silences in studies of emotion work', *Organizational Studies*, 24(5): 721–42.

Mirchandani, K. (2008) 'Challenging racial silences in studies of emotion work', in M. Greco and P. Stenner (eds) *Emotions: A Social Science Reader*, London: Routledge.

Moghadam, V.M. (1999) 'Gender and globalization: female labor and women's mobilization', *Journal of World-Systems Research*, 5(2): 367–88.

Mohammad, M. (2009) 'Politicization of Islam in Indonesia and Malaysia: women's rights and interreligious relations', in T.W. Devasahayam (ed.) *Gender Trends in Southeast Asia: Women Now, Women in the Future*, Singapore: Institute of Southeast Asian Studies.

Morgan, D.H.J. (1992) *Discovering Men*, London: Routledge.

Morris-Suzuki, T. (1998) 'Invisible countries: Japan and the Asian dream', *Asian Studies Review*, 22 (1): 1–22.

Mujahid, G. (2006) 'Population ageing in East and South-east Asia, 1950–2050: implications for elderly care', *Asia-Pacific Population Journal*, 21(2): 25–44.

Nagata, J.A. (1994) 'How to be Islamic without being an Islamic state', in A. Ahmed and H. Donnan (eds*)* *Islam, Globalization and Postmodernity*, London: Routledge.

Nakamatsu, T. (2005a) 'Faces of "Asian brides": gender, race and class in the representation of immigrant women in Japan', *Women's Studies International Forum*, 28: 405–17.

Nakamatsu, T. (2005b) 'Complex power and diverse responses: transnational marriage migration and women's agency', in L. Parker (ed.) *The Agency of Women in Asia*, Singapore: Marshall Cavendish.

Nam, J.-L. (1994) 'Women's role in export dependence and state control of labor unions in South Korea', *Women's Studies International Forum*, 17(1): 57–67.

National Authority for the Placement and Protection of Indonesian Overseas Workers (2007) Penempatan Tenaga Kerja Indonesia 1994–2007, 'Menurut Jenis Kelamin dan Negora Tujuan' (BNP2TK1). Online Available HTTP: http://www.bnp2tki.go.id/content/view/180/87/ (accessed 25 July 2010).

Nemoto, K. (2008) 'Postponed marriage: exploring women's views of matrimony and work in Japan', *Gender & Society*, 22(2): 219–37.

New Straits Times (2000) 'Strike balance between work and family, officers told', 19 October.

Newsweek (2008) 'Bottom of the barrel', 15 March.

Nonini, D.M. (1997) 'Shifting identities, positioned imaginaries: transnational traversals and reversals by Malaysian Chinese', in A. Ong and D.M. Nonini (eds) *Underground Empires: The Cultural Politics of Modern Chinese Transnationalism*, London: Routledge.

Oakley, A. (1974) *The Sociology of Housework*, London: Martin Robertson.

OECD (2002) *Babies and Bosses: Reconciling Work and Family Life*, Vol. 1, *Australia, Denmark and the Netherlands*, Paris: OECD.

OECD/KOREA Policy Centre (2009) *Society at a Glance* (Asia/Pacific Edition). Online Available HTTP: http://www.oecd.org/dataoecd/28/6/43463355.pdf (accessed 10 February 2010).

Office of the High Commissioner for Human Rights (2010) 'Regional Human Rights Context'. Online Available HTTP: http://www.ohchr.org/EN/Countries/AsiaRegion/Pages/AsiaPacificProgramme0809.aspx (accessed 1 March 2010).

Office of the United Nations High Commissioner for Human Rights (1996–2007a). Online Available HTTP: http://www2.ohchr.org/english/law/cmw.htm (accessed 1 March 2010).

Office of the United Nations High Commissioner for Human Rights (1996–2007b). Online Available HTTP: http://www2.ohchr.org/english/bodies/cmw/faqs.htm (accessed 1 March 2010).

Ogawa, N. (2002) 'Japan's changing fertility mechanism and its policy responses', paper presented at the International Workshop on Fertility Decline, Below Replacement Fertility and the Family in Asia: Prospects, Consequences and Policies, Singapore, April.

Ogawa, N., Lee, S.-H. and Matsukura, R. (2005) 'Health and its impact on work and dependency among the elderly in Japan', *Asian Population Studies*, 1(1): 121–45.

Oishi, N. (2005) *Women in Motion: Globalization, State Policies, and Labor Migration in Asia*, Stanford, CA: Stanford University Press.

Ong, A. (1987) *Spirits of Resistance and Capitalist Discipline: Factory Women in Malaysia*, Albany, NY: SUNY University Press.

Ong, A. (1990) 'Malay families, women's bodies and the body politic', *American Ethnologist*, 17(2): 28–42.

Ong, A. (1995) 'State versus Islam: Malay families, women's bodies, and the body politic in Malaysia', in A. Ong and M.G. Peletz (eds) *Bewitching Women, Pious Men: Gender and Body Politics in Southeast Asia*, Berkeley, CA: University of California Press.

Ong, A. (2006) *Neoliberalism as Exception: Mutations in Citizenship and Sovereignty*, Durham, NC: Duke University Press.

Ong, D. (2007) 'The career mother in matrimonial and custody proceedings in Singapore', in T.W. Devasahayam and B.S.A. Yeoh (eds) *Working and Mothering in Asia: Images, Ideologies and Identities*, Singapore and Denmark: National University of Singapore Press and Nordic Institute of Asian Studies.

Oostendorp, R.H. (2009) 'Globalization and the gender wage gap', *The World Bank Economic Review*, 23(1): 141–61.

Osaki, K. (1999) 'Economic interactions of migrants and their households of origin: are women more reliable supporters?', *Asian and Pacific Migration Journal*, 8: 447–71.

Panam, A., Khaing, M.K.Z., Caouette, T. and Punpuing, S. (2004) *Migrant Domestic Workers: From Burma to Thailand*, Nakhonpathom, Thailand: Institute for Population and Social Research.

Pearson, R. (1997) ' "Nimble fingers" revisited: reflections on women and third world industrialisation in the late twentieth century', in C. Jackson and R. Pearson (eds) *Feminist Visions of Development: Gender Analysis and Policy*, London: Routledge.

Pécoud, A. (2009) 'The UN Convention on migrant workers' rights and international migration management', *Global Society*, 23(3): 333–50.

Pécoud, A. and de Guchteneire, P. (2004) 'Migration, human rights and the United Nations: an investigation into the low ratification record of the UN Migrant Workers Convention', Global Migration Perspectives, No.3. Online Available HTTP: http://www.gcim. org/gmp/Global%20Migration%20Perspectives%20No%203.pdf (accessed 1 March 2010).

Pedrajas, T.P. (1997) 'Filipino maternal employment: its impact on self, husband, and children', in J. Frankel (ed.) *Families of Employed Mothers: An International Perspective*, New York: Garland Publishing.

Perrons, D. (2004) *Globalisation and Social Change*, London: Routledge.

Piderit, S. and Ashford, S. (2003) 'Breaking the silence: tactical choices women managers make in speaking up about gender issues', *Journal of Management Studies*, 40(6): 1477–502.

Pierce, J. (1995) *Gender Trials: Emotional Lives in Contemporary Law Firms*, Berkeley, CA: University of California Press.

Piper, N. (2003) 'Feminization of labor migration as violence against women', *Violence Against Women*, 9(6): 723–45.

Piper, N. (2004a) 'Gender and migration policies in Southeast and East Asia: legal protection and sociocultural empowerment of unskilled migrant women', *Singapore Journal of Tropical Geography*, 25(2): 216–31.

Piper, N. (2004b) 'Rights of foreign workers and the politics of migration in South-east and East Asia', *International Migration*, 42(5): 71–97.

Piper, N. and Roces, M (2003) 'Introduction: marriage and migration in an age of globalization', in N. Piper and M. Roces (eds) *Wife or Worker?: Asian Women and Migration*, Lanham, MD: Rowman & Littlefield Publishers.

Pocock, B. (2006) *The Labour Market Ate My Babies: Work, Children and a Sustainable Future*, Annandale, NSW: The Federation Press.

Prachuabmoh, V. and Mithranon, P. (2003) 'Below-replacement fertility in Thailand and its policy implications', *Journal of Population Research*, 20(1): 35–50.

Prieto-Carrón, M. (2008) 'Women workers, industrialization, global supply chains and corporate codes of conduct', *Journal of Business Ethics*, 83: 5–17.

Qu, L. and Weston, R. (2005) 'A woman's place: work hour preferences revisited', *Family Matters*, 72: 72–7.

Radelet, S. and Sachs, J. (1997) 'Asia's reemergence', *Foreign Affairs*. Online Available HTTP: http://www.earthinstitute.columbia.edu/sitefiles/file/about/director/documents/ar97.pdf (accessed 8 February 2010).

Radelet, S., Sachs, J. and Lee, J.-W. (1997) 'Economic growth in Asia', paper presented for the Asian Development Bank's study on Emerging Asia: Changes and Challenges. Online Available HTTP: www.cid.harvard.edu/archive/hiid/papers/ecgasia.pdf (accessed 10 October 2010).

Rahman, Md. M. and Lian, K.F. (2005) 'Bangladeshi migrant workers in Singapore: the view from inside', *Asia-Pacific Population Journal*, 20(1): 63–88.

Rahman, N.A. and Devasahayam, T.W. 'Motherhood: meanings on the move', paper presented at Working and Mothering: Asian Mothers Negotiating Family Work Challenges and Family Commitments, Singapore, January 2004.

Rama, M. (2002) 'The gender implications of public sector downsizing: the reform program of Viet Nam', *The World Bank Research Observer*, 17(2): 167–189.

Ranson, G. (2001) 'Men at work: change – or no change? –in the era of the "new fathers"', *Men and Masculinities*, 4(1): 3–26.

Rasiah, R. and Yun, H.I. (2009) 'Industrializing Southeast Asia', *Journal of the Asia Pacific Economy*, 14(2): 107–15.

Raymo, J.M. (2003) 'Educational attainment and the transition to first marriage among Japanese women', *Demography*, 40(1): 83–103.

Raymo, J.M. and Iwasawa, M. (2005) 'Marriage market mismatches in Japan: an alternative view of the relationship between women's education and marriage', *American Sociological Review*, 70(5): 801–22.

Raymo, J.M. and Iwasawa, M. (2008) 'Bridal pregnancy and spouse pairing patterns in Japan', *Journal of Marriage and Family*, 70: 847–60.

Raymo, J.M. and Ono, H. (2007) 'Coresidence with parents, women's economic resources, and the transition to marriage in Japan', *Journal of Family Issues*, 28(5): 653–81.

Reay, D. (2004) 'Gendering Bourdieu's concept of capitals? Emotional capital, women and social class', in L. Adkins and B. Skeggs (eds) *Feminism after Bourdieu*, Oxford: Blackwell Publishers.

Resurreccion, B.P. (2009) 'Gender trends in migration and employment in Southeast Asia', in T.W. Devasahayam (ed.) *Gender Trends in Southeast Asia: Women Now, Women in the Future*, Singapore: Institute of Southeast Asian Studies.

Rhode, D.L. (1997) *Speaking of Sex: The Denial of Gender Inequality*, Cambridge, MA: Harvard University Press.

Rinaldo, R. 'Engendering morality: women, Islam, and the nation-state in Indonesia', paper presented at the Gender Studies Seminar Series, Institute of Southeast Asian Studies, December 2008.

Robey, B. (ed.) (1989) 'Falling fertility in Indonesia: success in national family planning', *Asia Pacific Population & Policy*, December, No. 11. http:www.eastwestcenter.org/fileadmin/stored/pdfs/p&p011.pdf.

Robinson, K. and Bessell, S. (2002) 'Introduction to the issues', in K. Robinson and S. Bessell (eds) *Women in Indonesia: Gender, Equity and Development*, Singapore: Institute of Southeast Asian Studies.

Roth, L.M. (2001) 'Engendering sex-segregation: queuing and revolving doors on Wall Street', unpublished paper, University of Arizona.

Ruddick, S. (1998) 'Care as labor and relationship', in J.G. Haber and M.S. Halfon (eds)

Norms and Values: Essays on the Work of Virginia Held, Lanham, MD: Rowman & Littlefield.

Salazar Parreñas, R. (2000) 'Migrant Filipina domestic workers and the international division of reproductive labour', *Gender and Society*, 14: 560–80.

Salazar Parreñas, R. (2001a) *Servants of Globalization: Women, Migration and Domestic Work*, Stanford, CA: Stanford University Press.

Salazar Parreñas, R. (2001b) 'Mothering from a distance: emotions, gender, and intergenerational relations in Filipino transnational families', *Feminist Studies*, 27(2): 361–90.

Salazar Parrañes, R. (2005) *Children of Global Migration: Transnational Families and Gendered Woes*, Stanford, CA: Stanford University Press.

Sally, R. (2008) 'The political economy of trade-policy reform: lessons from developing countries', *The Journal of International Trade and Diplomacy*, 2(2): 55–96.

Sampang, C. (2005) *Maid in Singapore*, Singapore: Marshall Cavendish.

Sassen, S. (1998) *Globalization and its Discontents*, New York: New Press.

Sassen, S. (2000) 'Women's burden: counter-geographies of globalization and the feminization of survival', *Journal of International Affairs*, pp. 1–7. Online Available HTTP. http:www.allbusiness.com/government/3493201-1.html (accessed 11 October 2010).

Sassen, S. (2003) 'Global cities and survival circuits', in B. Ehrenreich and A.R. Hochschild (eds) *Global Woman: Nannies, Maids and Sex Workers in the New Economy*, New York: Metropolitan Books.

Satterthwaite, M.L. (2005) 'Crossing borders, claiming rights: using human rights law to empower women migrant workers', *Yale Human Rights & Development Law Journal*, 8(1): 1–74.

Schuck, P.H. (2000) 'Law and the study of migration', in C.B. Brettell and J.F. Hollifield (eds) *Migration Theory: Talking across Disciplines*, New York: Routledge.

Secondi, G. (1997) 'Private monetary transfers in rural China: are families altruistic?' *Journal of Development Studies*, 33(4): 487–511.

Securities Industry Association (SIA) (1998) G. Toto and G. Monohan (eds) *Fact Book*, New York: Securities Industry Association.

Sedgewick, E.K. (2003) *Touching, Feeling: Affect, Pedagogy, Performativity*, Durham, NC: Duke University Press.

Seguino, S. (1997) 'Gender wage inequality and export-led growth in South Korea', *Journal of Development Studies*, 34(2): 102–32.

Seguino, S. (2000) 'Accounting for gender in Asian economic growth', *Feminist Economics*, 6(3): 27–58.

Sen, G. (1994) 'Reproduction: the feminist challenge to social policy', in G. Sen and R.C. Snow (eds) *Power and Decision: The Social Control of Reproduction*, Boston: Harvard School of Public Health.

Sheller, M. and Urry, J. (2003) 'Mobile transformations of "public" and "private" life', *Theory, Culture and Society*, 20(3): 107–25.

Silva, E. (1999) 'Transforming housewifery: practices, dispositions and technologies', in E.B. Silva and C. Smart (eds) *The New Family*, London: Sage.

Silva, E. (2002) 'Routine matters: narratives of everyday life in families', in G. Crow and S. Heath (eds) *Social Conceptions of Time Structure and Process in Everyday Life*, Basingstoke: Palgrave.

Simpson, R. (1997) 'Have times changed? Career barriers and the token woman manager', *British Journal of Management*, 8: 121–9.

levels of the organization impacts on women managers', *Women in Management Review*, 15(11): 5–20.

Simpson, R. (2004) 'Masculinity at work: the experience of men in female dominated occupations', *Work, Employment, Society*, 18(2): 349–68.

Simpson, R. (2009) *Men in Caring Occupations: Doing Gender Differently*, Houndsmill: Palgrave Macmillan.

Simpson, R. and Lewis, P. (2005) 'An investigation of silence and a scrutiny of transparency: re-examining gender in organization literature through the concepts of voice and visibility', *Human Relations*, 58(10): 1253–75.

Skeggs, B. (1997) *Formations of Class and Gender: Becoming Respectable*, London: Sage.

Skeggs, B. (2004) 'Context and background: Pierre Bourdieu's analysis of class, gender and sexuality', in L. Adkins and B. Skeggs (eds) *Feminism after Bourdieu*, Oxford: Blackwell.

Sobritchea, C.I. (2007) 'Constructions of mothering: the experience of female Filipino overseas workers', in T.W. Devasahayam and B.S.A. Yeoh (eds) *Working and Mothering in Asia: Images, Ideologies and Identities*, Singapore and Denmark: National University of Singapore Press and Nordic Institute of Asian Studies.

'Southeast Asia – Migration News/Migration Dialogue' (2009) Overseas Filipino Workers (OFWS) in Taiwan, 25 May. Online Available HTTP: http://taiwanofws.blogspot.com/2009/05/southeast-asia-migration-news-migration.html (accessed 24 November 2009).

Stahl, C.W. (2003) 'International labour migration in East Asia: trends and policy issues', in R. Iredale, C. Hawksley and S. Castles (eds) *Migration in the Asia Pacific: Population, Settlement and Citizenship Issues*, Cheltenham: Edward Elgar.

Standing, G. (1976) 'Education and female participation in the labour force', *International Labour Review*, 114(3): 281–97.

Standing, G. (1989) 'Global feminization through flexible labour', *World Development*, 17(7): 1077–95.

Standing, G. (1999) 'Global feminization through flexible labor: a theme revisited', *World Development*, 27(3): 583–602.

Steinberg, R.J. and Figart, D. M. (1999) 'Emotional labour since *The Managed Heart*', *Annals of the American Academy of Political and Social Science*, 56(1): 8–26.

Stivens, M. (1996) *Matriliny and Modernity: Sexual Politics and Social Change in Rural Malaysia*, Sydney: Allen and Unwin.

Stivens, M. (1998a) 'Theorising gender, power and modernity in affluent Asia', in K. Sen and M. Stivens (eds) *Gender and Power in Affluent Asia*, London: Routledge.

Stivens, M. (1998b) 'Sex, gender and the Malay middle-class', in K. Sen and M. Stivens (eds) *Gender and Power in Affluent Asia*, London: Routledge.

Stivens, M. (2000) 'Re-inventing the "Asian family": "Asian values", globalization and cultural contest in Southeast Asia', paper presented at the Conference on Families in the Golden Age, Singapore, October.

Stivens, M. (2007) 'Postmodern motherhoods and cultural contest in Malaysia and Singapore', in T.W. Devasahayam and B.S.A. Yeoh (eds) *Working and Mothering in Asia: Images, Ideologies and Identities*, Singapore and Denmark: National University of Singapore Press and Nordic Institute of Asian Studies.

Sullivan, N. (1994) *Masters and Managers: A Study of Gender Relations in Urban Java*, Sydney: Allen & Unwin.

Sundquist, J. (2001) 'Migration, equality and access to health care services', *Journal of Epidemiology & Community Health*, 55: 691–2.

Tam, V.C.W. (1999) 'Foreign domestic helpers in Hong Kong and their role in childcare provision', in J.H. Momsen (ed.) *Gender, Migration and Domestic Service*, London: Routledge.

Tan, E.A. (2001) 'Labour market adjustments to large scale emigration: the Philippine case', *Asian and Pacific Migration Journal*, 2(3): 379–400.

Tenaganita, 'Maid abuse: housewife gets 18 years', 27 November 2008. Online Available HTTP: http://www.tenaganita.net/index.php?option=com_content&task=view&id=260 &Itemid=51 (accessed 22 January 2010).

Teo, Y. (2009) 'Gender disarmed: how gendered policies produce gender-neutral politics in Singapore', *Signs: Journal of Women in Culture and Society*, 34(3): 533–57.

The Malaysian Insider (2010) 'Jakarta wants KL to settle maid abuse cases promptly', 29 January 2010. Online Available HTTP: http://www.themalaysianinsider.com/ index.php/malaysia/41928-jakarta-wants-kl-to-settle-maid-abuse-cases-promptly (accessed 29 January 2010).

The Straits Times (2003) 'Window displays of maids must stop, agencies told', Ho, K. 15 October.

The Straits Times (2004) 'Sex-less in Singapore', 18 January, p. 25.

The Straits Times (2009a) 'Help with foreign workers' wage claims', 20 January. Online AvailableHTTP:http://www.twc2.org.sg/site/letters-to-the-press/response-to-the-straits-times-forum-page-2.html (accessed 28 January 2010).

The Straits Times (2009b) 'Jakarta stops sending maids to Malaysia from today', 26 June, p. A18.

The Sunday Times (2007) 'Sex and the single Vietnamese girl', 20 May, p. 31.

Thi, L. (1996) 'Women, marriage, family, and gender equality', in K. Barry (ed.) *Vietnam's Women in Transition*, Basingstoke and London: Macmillan Press.

Think Centre (2004) 'Indian migrant workers protest again', 17 July. Online Available HTTP: http://www.thinkcentre.org/article.cfm?ArticleID=2420 (accessed 28 January 2010).

Toyota, M. (2004) 'Health concerns of "invisible" foreign domestic maids in Thailand', Asian Metacentre Research Paper Series, No. 19, Singapore: National University of Singapore. Online Available HTTP: http://www.populationasia.org/Publications/RP/ AMCRP19.pdf (accessed 10 February 2010).

Tsai, P.-L. and Tsay, C.-L. (2004) 'Foreign direct investment and international labour migration in economic development: Indonesia, Malaysia, Philippines and Thailand', in A. Ananta and E.N. Arifin (eds) *International Migration in Southeast Asia*, Singapore: Institute of Southeast Asian Studies.

Turner, B.S. (1993) 'Contemporary problems in the theory of citizenship', in B.S. Turner (ed.) *Citizenship and Social Theory*, Newbury Park, CA: Sage Publications.

Turner, B.S. (2005) 'Citizenship, rights, and health care', in J. Germov (ed.) *Second Opinion: An Introduction to Health Sociology*, Melbourne: Oxford University Press.

Tyner, J.A. (2002) 'The globalization of transnational labor migration and the Filipino family: a narrative', *Asian and Pacific Migration Journal*, 11(1): 95–116.

UNFPA (2006) *UNFPA State of World Population*. http://www.unfpa.org/swp/2006/ English/chapter_3/toil_and_tears.html (accessed 10 February 2010).

UNIFEM (2005) 'The gender responsive budgeting policy of the Philippines'. Online Available HTTP: http://www.gender-budgets.org/content/view/35/124/ (accessed 10 February 2010).

UNIFEM (n.d.) 'Asia & the Pacific'. Online Available HTTP: http://www.unifem.org/ worldwide/asia_pacific/ (accessed 28 November 2009).

United Nations (2004) *Trade and Gender: Opportunities and Challenges for Developing Countries*, New York: United Nations.

United Nations (2006) *2004 World Survey on the Role of Women in Development: Women and International Migration* (/A/59/287/Add.1, ST/ESA/294), New York: Division for the Advancement of Women, Department of Economic and Social Affairs, United Nations.

United Nations (2009) *2009 World Survey on the Role of Women in Development: Women's Control over Economic Resources and Access to Financial Resources, Including Microfinance* (ST/ESA/326), New York: Division for the Advancement of Women, Department of Economic and Social Affairs, United Nations. Online Available HTTP: http://www.un.org/womenwatch/daw/public/worldsurvey2009.pdf (accessed 10 October 2010).

United Nations Development Programme (UNDP) (2008) *HIV Vulnerabilities of Migrant Women: From Asia to the Arab States*, Colombo, Sri Lanka: UNDP Regional Centre. Online Available HTTP: http://www2.undprcc.lk/resource_centre/pub_pdfs/P1105.pdf (accessed 28 January 2010).

United Nations Economic and Social Commission for Asia and the Pacific (UNESCAP) (2007) *Economic and Social Survey of Asia and the Pacific 2007: Surging Ahead in Uncertain Times*, Bangkok: Economic and Social Commission for Asia and the Pacific. Online Available HTTP: http://www.unescap.org/survey2007/download/O1_Survey-2007.pdf (accessed 13 October 2010).

United Nations Economic and Social Commission for Asia and the Pacific (UNESCAP) (2008) 'Key trends and challenges on international migration and development in Asia and the Pacific', paper presented at Expert Group Meeting on International Migration and Development in Asia and the Pacific, Population Division, Department of Economic and Social Affairs, Bangkok, September.

United Nations Educational, Scientific and Cultural Organization (2010) 'International Migration Convention'. Online Available HTTP: http://www.unesco.org/new/en/social-and-human-sciences/themes/social-transformations/international-migration/international-migration-convention/ (accessed 8 October 2010) .

'United Nations Treaty Collection' (2010a) 'International Convention on the Protection of the Rights of All Migrant Workers and their Families'. Online Available HTTP: http://treaties.un.org/Pages/ViewDetails.aspx?src=TREATY&mtdsg_no=IV-13&chapter=4&lang=en (accessed 28 March 2010).

'United Nations Treaty Collection' (2010b) 'Convention on the Elimination of All Forms of Discrimination Against Women'. Online Available HTTP: http://treaties.un.org/Pages/ViewDetails.aspx?src=TREATY&mtdsg_no=IV-8&chapter=4&lang=en (accessed 1 March 2010).

Vanwey, L.K. (2004) 'Altruistic and contractual remittances between male and female migrants and households in rural Thailand', *Demography*, 41(4): 739–56.

Wajcman, J. (1996) 'Women and men managers: careers and equal opportunities' in D.G. Crompton and K. Purcell (eds) *Changing Forms of Employment: Organizational Skills and Gender*, London: Routledge.

Watson, S. (1999) 'Policing the affective society: beyond governmentality in the theory of social control', *Social & Legal Studies*, 8: 227–51.

Wee, V. and Sim, A. (2004) 'Transnational networks in female labour migration in economic development: Indonesia, Malaysia, Philippines and Thailand', in A. Ananta and E. N. Arifin (eds) *International Migration in Southeast Asia*, Singapore: Institute of Southeast Asian Studies.

Weix, G.G. (2000) 'Inside the home and outside the family: the domestic estrangement of

Javanese servants', in K.M. Adams and S. Dickey (eds) *Home and Hegemony: Domestic Service and Identity Politics in South and Southeast Asia*, Ann Arbor, MI: University of Michigan Press.

White, S. (2006) 'Gender and the family', in G. Fealy and V. Hooker (eds) *Voices on Islam in Southeast Asia: A Contemporary Sourcebook*, Singapore: Institute of Southeast Asian Studies.

Whitehouse, G. and Hosking, A. (2005) 'Policy frameworks and parental employment: a comparison of Australia, the United States and the United Kingdom', paper presented at Transitions and Risk: New Directions in Social Policy Conference, Melbourne, 23–25 February.

Williams, C. (1993) *Doing Women's Work*, London: Sage.

Williams, J. (2000) *Unbending Gender: Why Family and Work Conflict and What to Do about It*, Oxford: Oxford University Press.

Willis, K. and Yeoh, B.S.A. (2000) 'Gender and transnational household strategies: Singaporean migration to China', *Regional Studies*, 34(3): 253–64.

Wong, C.K. (1992) 'Economic growth and welfare provision: the case of child day care in Hong Kong', *International Social Work*, 35: 389–404.

Wong, D. (1996) 'Foreign domestic workers in Singapore', *Asian and Pacific Migration Journal*, 5(1): 117–38.

Wong, T., Ng, E.K., Yeoh, B.S.A. and Khan, H.T.A. (2003) *Researching Migration and the Family*, Singapore: National University of Singapore/Asian MetaCentre for Population and Sustainable Development Analysis.

Wong, T., Yeoh, B.S.A., Graham, E.F. and Teo, P. (2004) 'Spaces of silence: single parenthood and the "normal family" in Singapore', *Population, Space and Place*, 10: 43–58.

World Economic Forum (2009) *The Global Gender Gap Report*, Geneva, Switzerland: World Economic Forum. Online Available HTTP: http://www.weforum.org/pdf/gendergap/report2009.pdf (accessed 8 January 2010).

Yap, M.T. (2002) 'Fertility and population policy: the Singapore experience', *Journal of Population and Social Security (Population)*, Supplement to Vol. 1: 643–58. Online Available HTTP: http://www.ipss.go.jp/webj-ad/webJournal.files/population/2003_6/24.Yap.pdf (accessed 26 February 2010).

Yarr, L.J. (1996) 'Gender and the allocation of time: impact on the household economy', in K. Barry (ed.) *Vietnam's Women in Transition*, New York: St Martin's Press.

Yea, S. (2005) 'When push comes to shove: sites of vulnerability, personal transformation, and trafficked women's migration decisions', *Sojourn: Journal of Social Issues in Southeast Asia*, 20(1): 67–95.

Yea, S. (2008) 'Married to the military: Filipinas negotiating transnational families', *International Migration*, 46(4): 111–44.

Yeo, E. (2004) 'Southeast Asia: images of migrants often negative—critics', *IPS*, as cited in Asian Labour News. Online Available HTTP: http://www.asianlabour.org/archives/003278.php (accessed 21 September 2005).

Yeoh, B.S.A (2005) 'Observations on transnational urbanism: possibilities, politics and costs of simultaneity', *Journal of Ethnic and Migration Studies*, 31(2): 409–13.

Yeoh, B.S.A. and Huang, S. (1995) 'Childcare in Singapore: negotiating choices and constraints in a multicultural society', *Women's Studies International Forum*, 18(4): 445–61.

Yeoh, B. and Huang, S. (1999) 'Spaces at the margins: migrant domestic workers and the development of civil society in Singapore', *Environment and Planning A*, 31(7): 1149–67.

Yeoh, B.S.A. and Huang, S. (2000) '"Home" and "away": foreign domestic workers and negotiations of diasporic identity in Singapore', *Women's Studies International Forum*, 23(4): 413–29.

Yeoh, B.S.A., Huang, S. and Devasahayam, T.W. (2004) 'Diasporic subjects in the nation: foreign domestic workers, the reach of the law and civil society in Singapore', *Asian Studies Review*, 28: 7–23.

Yeoh, B.S.A., Huang, S. and Gonzalez III, J. (1999) 'Migrant female domestic workers: debating the economic, social and political impacts in Singapore', *International Migration Review*, 33(1): 114–36.

Yeoh, B.S.A. and Khoo, L.-M. (1998) 'Home, work and community: skilled international migration and expatriate women in Singapore', *International Migration*, 36(2): 159–86.

Young, G., Fort, L. and Danner, M. (1996) 'Gender inequality in labor-force participation across nations (circa 1980)', in P.J. Dubeck and K. Borman (eds) *Women and Work: A Handbook*, New York: Garland Publishing.

Yu, W.-H. (2001) 'Family demands, gender attitudes, and married women's labor force participation: comparing Japan and Taiwan', in M.C. Brinton (ed.) *Women's Working Lives in East Asia*, Stanford, CA: Stanford University Press.

Zafarullah, H. (2000) 'Through the brick wall, and the glass ceiling: women in the civil service in Bangladesh', *Gender, Work and Organization*, 7(3): 197–209.

Zveglich, J.E. and Rodgers, Y.V.D.M. (2004) 'Occupational segregation and the gender wage gap in a dynamic East Asian economy', *Southern Economic Journal*, 70(4): 850–75.

Index

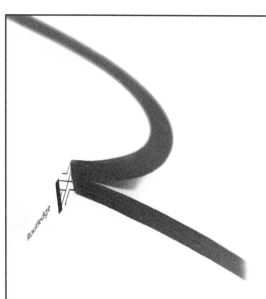

For Product Safety Concerns and Information please contact our EU
representative GPSR@taylorandfrancis.com Taylor & Francis Verlag GmbH,
Kaufingerstraße 24, 80331 München, Germany

Printed and bound by CPI Group (UK) Ltd, Croydon, CR0 4YY
01/05/2025
01858458-0001